Ladies of Spirit

A Comedy

Georgina Reid

A Samuel French Acting Edition

FOUNDED 1830

SAMUELFRENCH-LONDON.CO.UK
SAMUELFRENCH.COM

FOR AMATEUR PRODUCTION ENQUIRIES

UNITED KINGDOM AND WORLD
EXCLUDING NORTH AMERICA
plays@SamuelFrench-London.co.uk
020 7255 4302/01

Each title is subject to availability from Samuel French,

depending upon country of performance.

LADIES OF SPIRIT

SALLY BURGESS, *school secretary*
JANE COX ⎫
MRS. THORPE ⎪
MAY DANVERS ⎬ *teachers*
MISS MAUDESLEY ⎭
MISS ROWE, *headmistress*
MRS. EMMETT, *a parent*
MISS HARRIET PYE, *a former headmistress*
MISS MATILDA PYE, *her sister*

The action of the play takes place in the staff room at Gibraltar School, Hartmouth

ACT ONE *Late afternoon*

ACT TWO *Next morning*

ACT THREE *Next day, after school*

No character in this play is intended to portray any specific person, alive or dead.

ACT I

The staff room at Gibraltar School, Hartmouth. There is a long table C., with four seats drawn up to it. There is a large window, R., and above it a wardrobe. There is a door at back R., and another door U.L. U.L. and D.L. are cupboards and lockers. Noticeboard at back.

Enter SALLY *L. She is a pretty, feather-brained creature of twenty-two, gaily dressed in jumper and skirt. She carries a glass of water which she places at top right of table. She next fetches a fine chair with wooden arms and puts it at same place. There is pencil and paper at every place. She surveys her handiwork and counts the number of places silently. Seeing a pair of spectacles on table, she puts them on. draws in her chin, and looks round at the empty seats.*

SALLY (*solemnly*) Ladies, I have called this staff meeting because I am gravely displeased over a matter which affects the school very closely. It pains me to have to speak of it, but for the reputation of Gibraltar School I feel I must call attention to it. A very unfortunate situation has arisen. I am referring to last term's reports, or rather, to one report in particular. Angela Pursey's!

I find that Angela came bottom in every subject last term —with the exception of Domestic Science where she ate her cauliflower cheese before it could be judged. Bottom of the class, ladies, in every subject. Yes, I know somebody has to be bottom, but not Alderman Pursey's daughter! For years Alderman Pursey has supported this school with gifts of money. Without him we should lack many pleasing luxuries. How can you be so ungrateful as to place his daughter so low? Surely a little re-arrangement is all that is needed? The school motto? What has that to do with it? Yes, I know it means 'Keep to the Truth' but surely you can wrap it up differently! Think of the things that Angela is good at, and dwell on them. What is she good at? Oh come, there must be something. Telling tales?

Well, there you are, you could have said, 'Angela excels at Oral Composition'. After all, every child has an aptitude for something. You say she has an aptitude for eating three helpings of pudding? Well, couldn't you say, 'Takes a healthy interest in physical improvement'? I will send round another report for you to fill in, ladies, and this time I will cut off the school motto from the heading. I feel confident——

(*Enter* MISS ROWE, *the headmistress, from her room, U.R. She is an upright, well dressed woman of forty-five, with features that could be handsome, were it not for her cold eyes and grimly set mouth. Her voice rarely shows any emotion whatsoever.*)

MISS R What are you doing, Sally?

SALLY (*whipping off glasses*) Oh, Miss Rowe—I—I was preparing the table for the staff meeting.

MISS R And why the glass of water?

SALLY It's for you, Miss Rowe, in case your throat gets tired.

MISS R Quite unnecessary. I am not contemplating a filibuster. Kindly open the window. Someone has been smoking in here. (*She goes out L.*)

(SALLY *opens window a little, then goes to bookshelf U.C., and takes out dictionary. She goes and sits at right of table leafing it through in search of a word.*)

SALLY File—filial—filibeg—(*Raises eyebrows as she repeats this one.*) filibeg?—ah, filibuster. (*She reads and appears to find understanding.*) Oh. (*She reads on and becomes absorbed in the dictionary.*)

(*Enter* JANE COX, *an outspoken young woman of twenty-eight, and* MRS. THORPE, *a comfortable, rather shabby matron of forty. Both carry books which they dump on the table.* MRS. THORPE *flops into easy chair, D.L., kicking off her shoes.*)

JANE (*as she enters*) Well, I think it's a bit thick, to call a staff meeting on the very first day of term. I always said that woman wasn't human. No wonder the girls call her 'Hard Rowe'.

MRS. T The first day always seems interminable, anyway, without one of her stupid wrangling sessions.

JANE (*kneeling in front of cupboard D.L. to put her books away*) I don't know why she bothers to ask our opinion when she never pays any heed, just goes grimly ahead. I wonder what she's hatching up this time.

MRS. T You can be sure it's nothing to our advantage. Teachers are less than the dust in this dump. (*Looks at wrist watch.*) I wish she'd hurry up. I've to meet Timothy out of school and get him to the barber's. Yesterday somebody mistook him for a girl. (*Passes pile of books to* JANE.) Shove my load of rubbish in with yours, duckie. I'm not marking them till I've got to.

(*Enter* MISS MAUDESLEY, *a sweet-faced, gentle person of sixty-one.*)

MAUDIE I hope I'm not late.

MRS. T No, no.

MAUDIE I was drawing the Stuart family tree on the board, ready for tomorrow's lesson with 3B. They seem to have the greatest difficulty in distinguishing between Charles the first and Charles the second.

JANE Nell Gwynn never had any trouble. (*She crosses to R. and lights a cigarette.*)

MAUDIE (*smiling at her*) That's rather a pleasant little joke, Jane. Do you mind if I try it out on 3B?

JANE No, go ahead.

MAUDIE They respond so readily to a touch of humour but I'm not at all gifted in that line.

MRS. T Did you have nice holidays, Maudie?

MAUDIE Very nice, dear. Leamington is a charming town, I consider. And did you have a pleasant time?

MRS. T Riotous. Simply riotous. If you've never spent a wet week in a caravan with a case of measles, you haven't lived.

MAUDIE Timothy had measles?

MRS. T He did, the demon. But he survived and is now in the pink of condition, if his growth of hair is anything to go by.

SALLY (*looking up*) Is it flavescent, Mrs. Thorpe?

MRS. T Eh?

SALLY Timothy's hair. Is it flavescent?

JANE The dear girl's been reading the dictionary again. Come on, tell us what it means.

SALLY It means, 'turning yellow'. I'm going to memorise it. It could be useful in all sorts of conversations.

JANE Yes, perhaps we'll have an epidemic of jaundice.

SALLY —and I could ring up the doctor and tell him we're all flavescent!

MRS. T By the way, Maudie, I brought you back a little souvenir. Open it quickly before Blossom arrives. (*Gives her small packet.*) I don't want her to know or she'll think I ought to have brought her one too.

MAUDIE (*opening it*) How very kind.

JANE Huh! I wouldn't give May Danvers a sixpenny stick of rock.

MRS. T Something tells me you don't love our may-blossom.

JANE In the three months I have been at this school——

MAUDIE Oh, how pretty! Thank you so much, Mrs. Thorpe. I don't think I've ever had such a pretty brooch. See how it sparkles, Jane. I love shiny things. But you shouldn't have spent your money on me, you know.

MRS. T Oh goodness, it didn't cost much. But I know you're fond of brooches and trinkets.

MAUDIE Yes, indeed. I'll just pop into the cloakroom and try it on. (*She goes out L.*)

JANE Poor old dear. How thrilled she is.

SALLY I don't suppose she gets many presents.

JANE I wish I'd thought of getting her something. I am a selfish brute.

MRS. T Yes, all unmarried people are basically selfish. I was the same until Herbert took me unto him.

JANE (*with friendly scorn*) Complacent female! Maudie must be at least sixty, by now.

MRS. T Yes. She was here in the days of the two Misses Pye.

JANE That's the two old dears whose portraits hang side by side in the Assembly Hall, isn't it?

SALLY Yes. They started this school, you know. They ran it jointly for twenty years. Everybody in Hartmouth knew the two Misses Pye of Gibraltar School. Miss Hatty was the thin one with straight hair, and she always used an ebony cane to walk with, because of her arthritis. Miss Matty was the plump one with curly hair and dimples, and she had a big bunch of keys at her waist. They both died of influenza in January nineteen thirty-six.

JANE How come you know so much about them?

SALLY You forget that before I was the school secretary, I was a pupil here for seven years——

JANE So you were.

SALLY —and morning after morning, as I stood in that hall lisping my girlish prayers and listening to Hard Rowe's boring talks on growing up, I used to study those two portraits until I knew every detail. I could tell you how many buttons on their bodices or tucks on their sleeves. In the end it was as if I'd known them personally for years. There was a sort of gleam in Miss Hatty's eye, that seemed to look down on Miss Rowe and say, 'Cut the cackle, woman, and don't be such a bore.'

MRS. T You were obviously the sort of little girl who indulged in charming fantasies instead of attending to her teachers.

SALLY You're so right. When I finally left school I was appalled at the amount of knowledge I didn't know. That's why I'm putting in a bit of work with the dictionary. Better late than never.

JANE But if you're really so ignorant, and I must admit I've noticed it, how on earth did you get the job of school secretary? Are you related to Alderman Pursey or something?

SALLY Certainly not. It's simply because I answer the telephone so beautifully. Perfect elocution and unshakeable politeness are the only two things a girl learns in this school.

JANE Oh, don't exaggerate.

MRS. T She's not. (Chuckles.) Sally is a typical product of Gibraltar School. Her spelling is infantile, her punctuation non-existent and her arithmetic would disgrace a child of ten. She is totally unfitted for the job she holds and the things she does to my register are unforgiveable—but you should hear her talk to irate parents on the telephone. It's without parallel.

SALLY Parallel! (Opens dictionary eagerly.) I never know how to spell that one.

JANE You do depress me, Thorpey. I thought Gibraltar School had a fine reputation.

MRS. T So it did, once. But for ten years Miss Rowe has been happily guiding it downhill; economising on important things, employing unqualified teachers like me, because we're cheap; spending extravagantly on things we don't need, such as the trampoline in the gymnasium; pandering to the snob element of the town—

SALLY Pandering? I've just come to that. It says here, to pander is to minister to lust or passion.

MRS. T That wasn't the way I meant it, dear. It's a word you have to be very careful over.

SALLY Oh, one of those.

MRS. T Yes, one of those.

(*Enter* MISS ROWE *and* MISS DANVERS L. MAY DANVERS *is a few years younger than* MISS ROWE, *elegantly dressed and inclined to gush when not being actively unpleasant.* MRS. THORPE *puts on her shoes. They all rise and* SALLY *puts dictionary on edge of table* L.)

MISS R (*going to the big chair,* U.R.) Sit down, ladies, at the table. Miss Danvers here, being senior assistant. (*Points to seat beside her.*)

MAY Certainly, Miss Rowe. (*They all sit.*)

MISS R Is someone missing?

MRS. T Miss Maudesley was here but she had to slip out for a minute.

MISS R I see. Sally, you will sit over there and take notes so that a copy of the proceedings may be sent to the part time staff.

(SALLY *sits* D.R. *and gets out pad and pencil.*)

Miss Cox, while we are waiting for Miss Maudesley, may I have your attention?

JANE Of course.

MISS R I have just been talking to Angela Pursey. It seems you made her stay behind and finish an exercise.

JANE I did. She'd wasted all the lesson passing notes to other girls.

MISS R You must find some other form of correction. Angela is not to be kept in.

JANE May one ask why?

MISS R (*surprised at this sign of rebellion*) Angela is Alderman Pursey's daughter.

JANE I know she is. So what?

MISS R If I understand your American idiom, you require further elucidation?

(SALLY *reaches out desperately for the dictionary.*)

There is no need to take this down, Sally. The meeting has not started yet. Now, Miss Cox, since you have only been here for one term, you may not know that Alderman Pursey is a very influential man and a member of the Board of Governors. Every afternoon he sends his chauffeur to pick up Angela and drive her home. Alderman Pursey cannot spare his car and his chauffeur for unlimited periods while you keep his daughter after school hours. I'm sure you understand.

(JANE *looks angry and is about to speak when* MAUDIE *comes in* L.)

MAUDIE Oh, I'm sorry to keep you waiting.

MISS R Just take that seat, Miss Maudesley, and allow us to commence.

(MAUDIE *slips meekly into last seat,* L.C.)

MISS R Now, to work. I have several small items to announce. The first is a change in the name of the school. The Board of Governors and myself have decided to re-name the school 'Cedar Grove'. The previous name, 'Gibraltar School', was decidedly odd and had no apparent connection with a school for young ladies.

MAUDIE But it did have a connection. Miss Harriet and Miss Matilda were both born and brought up in Gibraltar. Their father was a naval captain. And besides, Miss Harriet used to say that a good education was a rock to build on, like the Rock of Gibraltar.

MISS R I dare say she did, but that was all a long time ago. We must move with the times.

MAY I think 'Cedar Grove' is a charming name.

MRS. T I always thought 'Gibraltar School' was a rather charming name.

MAY But it doesn't look like the Rock of Gibraltar.

JANE It doesn't look much like a Cedar Grove either. We have only one small cedar tree.

MAY Well, we can plant some more.

MAUDIE The Misses Pye would have hated it.

MAY The Misses Pye are no longer with us. What they'd think doesn't really count, Maudie darling.

MISS R All this discussion is pointless. The decision has been made. Here is a specimen copy of the new prospectus, sent to me from the printers' today. (*Passes it to* MAY, *on her L.*) Handle it carefully, please, as I have only the one.

MAY It looks very elegant, I must say. (*Passes it to* MAUDIE.)

MAUDIE (*with a sigh*) Whatever would Miss Harriet say? (*Passes it to* JANE.)

JANE Well, I think it's a pity. I liked the old name. (*Passes it to* MRS. THORPE.)

SALLY So did I. When I was at school, we used to call ourselves the Apes of the Rock!

MRS. T (*who has been studying the prospectus*) I see that the school fees have gone up another ten pounds a term.

MISS R Yes.

MRS. T Can we therefore hope for a rise in salary?

MISS R I'm afraid not. The money is needed to keep pace with the ever rising cost of upkeep and maintenance. However, that is a point which in no way concerns the teaching staff.

MRS. T I feel that it does. In this way, Miss Rowe. Over the last two years the fees have already gone up by fifty pounds per annum. Now you have added another thirty. This will put an immense strain on some of the parents and a few girls may have to leave. Already we draw our girls almost entirely from the upper strata of Hartmouth.

MISS R I fail to see that that is a cause for regret.

MRS. T I'm sorry, but I disagree. Plenty of money does not guarantee plenty of brains. Money won't get girls through their G.C.E. and our results over the past few years have been far from commendable.

MISS R I am obliged to you for pointing that out to me.

MRS. T What I feel is, well, now Hartmouth schools are going comprehensive, a lot of parents who disapprove of the system would like to send their daughters here if they could afford it. It could be greatly to our advantage.

MISS R What you say may be true, but I am anxious not to lower the tone of Gib—of Cedar Grove—by admitting girls from the poorer classes. I feel I owe it to the parents of my gently-reared pupils, not to allow them to mix with girls of common breeding.

JANE Gently reared, are they? Then I wonder who carved a certain word on the lavatory door?

MAY Well, since you raise the question, I reckon it was Susie Emmett.

JANE Oh no, Susie would never——

MISS R Susan Emmett is a case in point. She comes from a broken home and her background is not at all good. I consider her a bad influence in the school and I shall not be sorry if the rise in fees forces her to leave.

JANE But Susie has the best brain in the school! Her G.C.E. results next summer are going to be splendid.

SALLY And she can't have written that word in the lavatory because it isn't even spelt right!

MISS R We are straying from the point, which was the rise in fees. I am sure that you have only the remotest conception (SALLY *looks hungrily at the dictionary but* MRS. THORPE *is leaning on it.*)
of what it costs to run the school. Why, the swimming bath alone costs twenty pounds a week to keep the water warm and filtered.

JANE But we've got the sea on our doorstep. They could bathe in that for nothing.

MISS R Alderman Pursey donated the swimming bath. Then there are always pieces of apparatus needed. And we get no state aid, so you see the strictest economy must be practised. One of those economies is going to affect you all to a certain degree.
(*They look at each other warily.*)
You know that our P.E. mistress had to leave last term. We have decided that in future we will only employ a part time games mistress. The Physical Education will have

to be shared out among the full time staff. I am sure I can rely on your loyalty to give up one free period a week to that, ladies?

MAY Of course you can, Miss Rowe. It'll be rather fun after the inactivity of maths lessons.

MISS R Thank you, Miss Danvers. Miss Cox?

JANE Well, yes, I don't mind taking P.E., though it will only leave me with two free periods for doing my marking.

MISS R Many teachers take their marking home, Miss Cox.

MRS. T Well, that's something I don't intend to do. If I must take P.E. then I must, and it can't do any harm to my figure— but I'm taking no books home to mark. I've a family to feed and care for and a house to keep clean. If I don't get enough free periods to do my marking, the books will go unmarked.

MISS R Heaven forbid that I should disrupt your domesticity.
(SALLY *looks worried and chews her pencil.*)

MAY If I might make a suggestion, I often find time in the dinner hour to catch up on some marking.

MISS R Admirable. I'm sure Mrs. Thorpe will follow your example. And you, Miss Maudesley? I suppose you are willing to take a turn at Physical Education?

MAUDIE (*aghast*) Me? I—I——

JANE (*startled*) But surely Miss Maudesley won't be expected to take P.E.?

MISS R Why not, Miss Cox?

JANE Well—well, to put it bluntly, she's too old, surely!

MISS R (*blandly, to* MAUDIE) Are you, Miss Maudesley? Are you too old?

MAUDIE (*miserably, trying to sound brave*) Not at all, Miss Rowe. I'm sure I shall enjoy it.
(MAY *smiles sourly and the other teachers look dumb-founded.*)

MISS R Then that's settled. The new timetable will be ready to-morrow morning. I think that concludes most of the business. Have you got it all down, Sally?

SALLY Sort of—I mean—here and there. I mean—— Yes, Miss Rowe.

MISS R Good.

(*She rises and they follow suit.*)
Then before you go, I want you all to take a look in my room.

JANE (*mystified*) In your room? What for?

MISS R (*smiling primly*) On the wall you will see a wonderful oil painting by a brilliant young artist. It has been donated to the school by Alderman Pursey.

MAY Fancy that. How kind of him!

MISS R It is more than kind. I believe the painting cost him two hundred pounds.

MRS. T This I must see.

MISS R Please do.

(*The four teachers, led by* MRS. THORPE, *go through door on R.*)
Pass me your notes, Sally, and I'll check them over before you type them.
(SALLY *gives them unwillingly.*)
Hm. It seems as though you deliberately leave out the most important word in every sentence. (*She inserts a word here and there.*) And there's no need to make notes on every little aside. Erase all that about the word on the lavatory wall. One shouldn't dwell on vulgarity.

SALLY But isn't it hard not to when it stares you in the eye every time you—

MISS R Quite. And isn't it time you knew that grammar and commendable have two 'm's?

SALLY (*confused*) Do you mean four, Miss Rowe?

MISS R (*controlling an impulse to be rude*) Yes, Sally. Two each.

SALLY Yes, Miss Rowe.

MISS R See that it's typed out in triplicate first thing in the morning. That's all, I think. Do you want to go in and look at the painting?

SALLY I've seen it, Miss Rowe. I was in there when they brought it.

MISS R And what did you think of it?

SALLY (*trying to sound intelligent*) Well, it—it's rather flavescent, isn't it?

MISS R (*impressed*) Do you think so?

SALLY Oh yes, quite noticeably.

(*Enter* MAY *and* MAUDIE, U.R. MAUDIE *looks unhappy.* MAY *is all charm and gush.*)

MAY Oh Miss Rowe, it's wonderful. So colourful. So full of atmosphere. You are lucky to have it in your room.

MISS R Oh, make no mistake, I'm not keeping a masterpiece like that shut away in my room. As soon as possible I'm going to have it hung in the Assembly Hall, above the platform.

MAY Next to the Misses Pye?

MISS R The Pye sisters will have to come down, I'm afraid, and go into the chemistry lab. Such old fashioned stuff would look dreadful against a modern work of art.

MAUDIE (*rather desperately*) Oh no! Not the chemistry lab!

MISS R Why not the chemistry lab?

MAUDIE Miss Matilda couldn't stand chemistry. The smells made her feel sick.

MISS R Oh really, Miss Maudesley, I've no time for such childishness. Please do not be so obstructive. Now I must go and examine a cracked window in Room Three. (*She goes out L.*)

MAUDIE (*sitting despondently* D.L.) Oh dear, all these changes.

MAY You must move with the times, Maudie. It's no good expecting life to stand still. Personally, I'm all for a bit of change.
(*Enter* JANE *and* MRS. THORPE U.R.)

MRS. T Has she gone? That's good. I'd hate her to ask me what I thought of it.

SALLY She asked me. I said I thought it was rather flavescent.

JANE Good for you. I'd have called it putrescent.

SALLY What does that mean?

JANE It stinks. Ye Gods, two hundred pounds for that tasteless daub—and the Geography maps are falling to pieces. (*SALLY goes out U.R.*)

MRS. T (*getting her hat and coat from cupboard R.*) It's very interesting, really. It's exactly like paintings done by a child of six whom I used to teach, years ago.

JANE It might be the same boy. Did he grow up to be an artist?

MRS. T I don't think so. (*Puts on hat.*) The last I heard of him, he was in Borstal.

JANE (*grinning*) It's obviously the same bloke. (*Gets her hat and coat from cupboard, also* MAUDIE's.) Here, Maudie, here's your hat and coat.

(MAUDIE *turns her head away and does not answer.*)
Maudie, what's the matter?

MAY (*scornfully*) She's crying, I expect.

JANE (*dismayed*) Oh no! Maudie, you're not crying, are you?
(MAUDIE *fumbles for her handkerchief and shakes her head.*
JANE *kneels beside her.*)

MAY It's because Miss Rowe is going to hang that picture in the hall and put her precious Pye sisters in the chemmy lab.

JANE (*with an arm round the silently weeping* MAUDIE) Don't be silly. It's because of this wretched P.E. that we've all got to take—isn't it, Maudie? (MAUDIE *nods.*) Oh, it's outrageous to expect an elderly teacher to take a turn at that.

MAUDIE I used to take drill with the girls when I first came here——

MAY Drill! I ask you!

MAUDIE —but when I was in my forties I had an operation and Miss Harriet said I wasn't to take it any more. She was always so thoughtful for her staff.

MRS. T That's more than you can say for our present headmistress. But, honestly Maudie, why don't you stand up for yourself a bit more, instead of letting her browbeat you?

JANE Yes, why didn't you say straight out. 'I'm too old', when she asked you?

MAUDIE Jane dear, you don't understand. Miss Rowe knows that I'm sixty-one years old and the retirement age is sixty. If I don't do everything she requires of me, then she can get the School Board to force me to retire.

MAY (*who has found a newspaper in the cupboard and started reading it*) Well, isn't it time you retired?

MAUDIE I can't afford to. I have to support my invalid mother and I dare not give up until I've finished paying off the mortgage on our house.

MRS. T Well, cheer up, you don't have to do much in P.E., except shout at the girls and keep them on the run. I shan't budge from one spot when it's my turn.

MAUDIE But I can't make myself heard, out of doors. The girls will just laugh at me. And I'm sure to catch bronchitis.

B

JANE I tell you what. I'll do your P.E. lesson if you will take one of my English periods. I don't mind a bit.

MAUDIE (*hopefully*) Do you think she'd let you?

JANE I don't see why not. I'll speak to her in the morning.

MRS. T Now put on your hat and coat and I'll run you home in the car. Timothy will have given up waiting and gone to the park.

MAUDIE (*putting on clothes*) You are kind, really. I'm sorry I was so silly. It's all these changes coming so suddenly, that upset me. It won't be like the old school any more. It's a wonder Miss Hatty and Miss Matty don't turn in their graves.

MRS. T (*as they go off L.*) Yes, I expect they've done a few turns in the last half hour.

MAY (*scornfully*) Miss Hatty and Miss Matty! I ask you! It's like some dreadful Music Hall turn. Personally I shall be glad to have their portraits taken down. They give me the creeps looking down on us like a couple of old witches.

JANE (*distantly*) Do they? (*She starts to put on her coat.*)
    (MAY *goes on reading paper, perching on side of big table. Suddenly she sees something that startles her and she stands up.*)

MAY Wow! Look at that!

JANE (*still distantly*) Look at what?

MAY This photo. (*She holds up paper and* JANE *looks briefly.*)

JANE The latest pop singer in a vulgar satin dress?

MAY You don't recognise her?

JANE (*barely taking a second look*) Looks a bit like Susan Emmett.

MAY That's not surprising. It is Susan Emmett!

JANE (*startled at last*) What! It can't be!

MAY It says so. Listen. 'The Palais de Danse is very popular these days since charming young singer Susie Emmett joined the band. As our photograph shows, Susie has more than just a pretty voice to attract the boys'—and it certainly does show, doesn't it?

JANE But she's only fifteen. How perfectly awful. Whatever is her mother thinking about?

MAY Probably her mother put her up to it. She's as common

as mud. It's obviously one of her dresses that she's cut down for Susan. 'Cut down' is right too.

JANE (*very distressed*) It's wicked. To take a nice normal child of fifteen and dress her up with lipstick and satin and split skirt like any tart, and then let her sing in a dance hall late at night—no wonder she's been looking pale in the mornings.

MAY That's nothing to how she's going to look when Miss Rowe finds out.

JANE (*aghast*) You're not going to show this to Miss Rowe?

MAY I certainly am. She has a right to know.

JANE No she hasn't. What a person does in her private life is nobody's concern. It may be vulgar and foolish, and somebody needs to talk to her about it—but not Miss Rowe!

MAY Who then? You, I suppose?

JANE Well, all right. I'd be glad to. Susie's in my form and we get on well together.

MAY (*nastily*) Yes, I've noticed how friendly you are.

JANE (*getting angry*) What do you mean?

MAY Nothing. Nothing. But I am going to show this to Miss Rowe.

JANE No, May. Think what trouble she'll get into. Don't you see, this is just what Miss Rowe's looking for: an excuse to get rid of Susie altogether.

MAY And good riddance I say. Nasty common little slut.

JANE (*really angry*) She's nothing of the sort. She's—she's a sweet innocent child of very high intelligence.

MAY (*sarcastically, waving paper*) Yes, it looks like it, doesn't it?

JANE She doesn't understand how it looks.

MAY (*viciously*) She understands all right. I know her type, over-developed and over-sexed. All sugar and spice on the surface and a filthy mind underneath. Can't keep away from the men, even at that age. We don't want that sort here, spreading her poison among decent girls.

JANE My word, it isn't Susan who has the filthy mind around here. You'd better be careful, May Danvers. I'm not a poor, timid, old soul like Maudie, and I don't laugh things off with a shrug like Mrs. Thorpe. If you show that picture to the headmistress I shall tell her one or two things I know about your private life.

MAY (*uncertainly*) You don't know anything about me.

JANE Don't I? What if I told her——

(*They break off as* MISS ROWE *appears in doorway* L.)

MISS R Still there, ladies? Was there something you wanted to see me about?

JANE (*firmly*) No, Miss Rowe. We're just going, aren't we, Miss Danvers?

MAY (*after a moment*) Yes, of course.

(*She leaves the newspaper hopefully on table, and gets coat from cupboard. As she turns to go,* JANE *picks up paper and hands it to her.* MAY *takes it angrily and marches out* L.)

JANE Good afternoon, Miss Rowe.

MISS R Good afternoon.

(JANE *goes out* L. *Enter* SALLY R., *wearing coat and carrying typescript which she hands to* MISS ROWE.)

SALLY I've finished the notes on the staff meeting, Miss Rowe. Is it all right if I go now?

MISS R Yes, but I'd like you here early tomorrow morning to shift your things and mine into this room. One of the girls can help you with heavy stuff.

SALLY (*mystified*) Everything, Miss Rowe?

MISS R Yes. I am having my room redecorated. Pargeter and Son are arriving at nine o'clock tomorrow morning, so you and I will have to live in here for a week.

SALLY Crumbs! What about the telephone?

MISS R I think the cable is long enough to reach through the door if it were to stand here, on the little table. I don't suppose the staff will enjoy having us here—however they'll have to realise that we don't enjoy it much either.

SALLY (*thoughtlessly*) Oh, I shall. It'll be much more cheerful.

MISS R (*chilly*) Cheerful?

SALLY I mean, the sun comes in here more than in your room. Haven't you noticed?

MISS R Yes, but I am not emotionally influenced by it. Now, off you go. I have one or two more things to attend to. A headmistress's work is never done.

SALLY I'm glad I don't have to stay behind on my own. Empty buildings give me the creeps.

MISS R Indeed. Why?

SALLY Oh, I don't know. I think of the people who lived there once, and died long ago. Silly, aren't I?

MISS R Remarkably. Good afternoon, Sally.

SALLY Good afternoon, Miss Rowe.

(SALLY *goes out* L. MISS ROWE *looks around her, mentally re-arranging the room. She sweeps some books off the table and puts them on cupboard, D.L. She goes into her own room, U.R., and re-appears carrying telephone which she places on small table near door. She goes off R. again and shortly re-appears carrying handbag and telephone directory. She searches in her bag for a newspaper cutting (the photo of* SUSIE), *and places it on table beside the phone. Then she draws up a small chair and searches in directory for a number. On finding it, she dials the number and while waiting for an answer she reads the newspaper cutting with a look of distaste.*)

MISS R Hello. Is that Mrs. Emmett? This is Miss Rowe, your daughter's headmistress. . . I am well, thank you. I should be obliged if you could come and call on me in the near future as I have something I wish to discuss with you. . . . It is not a subject that I care to discuss over the telephone, Mrs. Emmett. Can I expect you tomorrow morning at ten o'clock? . . . I am aware that it may interfere with your plans but I think you would be well advised to attend. It concerns your daughter's future. . . . Thank you. I will expect you at ten. Goodbye. (*She replaces phone and sits for a moment with a grim smile. Then she goes and sits down at large table, picks up the new prospectus and admires it, then opens her handbag and gets out her fountain pen to correct* SALLY's *typed notes. The stage is getting darker and a faint greenish light is cast over the room. She does not look up when two elderly ladies enter the room, U.R. They are dressed in old-fashioned black garments and they move with a silent, gliding movement. The thinner one is* MISS HATTY, *the plump one,* MISS MATTY. MATTY *has a rather girlish, breathless way of speaking.*

HATTY *is more commanding and incisive. She often has to correct her sister, but she is never coldly repressive, like* MISS ROWE. *There is a humorous tone even in her most acid remarks, and toward her sister she is rather indulgent. They go and sit on opposite sides of the table and stare at* MISS ROWE *who is between them, working on, oblivious of their scrutiny.*)

MATTY (*in a whisper, after a long pause*) Hatty! She can't see us!

HATTY (*clearly*) There's no need to whisper, Matty. She can neither see us nor hear us. As far as she is concerned, we might as well not be here.

MATTY Oh, Hatty, when you say that, I feel sort of—dead!

HATTY You are dead, Matty. It's time you got used to it.

MATTY I thought I was used to it, but it took me by surprise when you told me the time had come to walk.

HATTY I couldn't stand by any longer, doing nothing while this wretched woman wrecks our life's work and turns our beloved school into a mockery. The changes she has threatened in the last half hour would make the laziest ghost walk.

MATTY Yes indeed. 'Cedar Grove'. I ask you! And putting poor Maudie on drill—I mean P.T.

HATTY P.E. And that picture is the last straw. I will not be relegated to the chemistry lab. to make room for a painting which I can only describe as—Tripe!

MATTY You describe it so well, dear. It certainly isn't worth two hundred pounds. Alderman Pursey would have done better to have installed some more wash basins in the cloakroom.

HATTY (*contemptuously*) Alderman Pursey, indeed! I remember young Oliver Pursey when he was a grubby little demon with a running nose.

MATTY (*giggling*) So do I. I remember the time he shouted rude names after you and you chased him up the road and boxed his ears.

HATTY (*sighing*) Yes. I was more sprightly then.
(MISS ROWE *has trouble with her pen.*)

MATTY What's she doing now?

HATTY Her pen has no more ink in it.
(MISS ROWE *looks around table for bottle of ink, then rises*

and looks on shelf U.C. While her back is turned, MISS
MATTY *reaches for ink bottle which was on window ledge
D.R., and puts it on table.* MISS ROWE *turns, sees bottle, is
amazed, sits and fills pen.*)
You shouldn't do things like that, Matty.

MATTY I was only trying to be helpful.

HATTY We're not here to help, only to hinder.

MATTY Oh yes, of course. When are we going to start?

HATTY Tomorrow, probably. I haven't made my plan of campaign
yet. I just wanted to have a good look at the woman.
Most of the time I can only see the top of her head, looking down from the wall of the assembly hall.

MATTY She's better looking than I expected.

HATTY Nobody can be good looking without a spark of warmth
and humanity about them. (*Rises.*) Come along, Matty,
we'd better get some rest if we're to start haunting tomorrow.
(*She makes for the door L., but* MATTY *lingers, yearningly.*)

MATTY Hatty, couldn't I just—make a start today?

HATTY In what way?

MATTY That prospectus—with the new name, Cedar Grove—it's
the only copy she's got and it's very nicely placed——

HATTY (*smiling a bit*) Oh, very well.
(MATTY *hovers until* MISS ROWE *reaches out towards the
open ink pot. Quickly,* MATTY *tips over the pot and ink
flows all over the prospectus.* MATTY *and* HATTY *go out,
smiling, L.* MISS ROWE *leaps to her feet and blots frantic-
ally with her handkerchief at the ruined prospectus.*)

CURTAIN

ACT II

Next morning. The scene is the same except that the big table has been moved further to the L., and a sofa has been placed D.R., under the window. SALLY's *typewriter is on small table beside the 'phone, at the back.*

HATTY *and* MATTY *are sitting on the sofa in an upright, waiting position.* MRS. EMMETT *is seated at L. of table on edge of upright chair, also waiting. She is a smartly dressed, over-made-up woman of about forty-two with sharp features and a hard voice.*

After a moment of silence, MATTY *speaks.*

MATTY Hatty, who is this woman?

HATTY The secretary called her Mrs. Emmett. She's waiting to see the headmistress.

MATTY What about?

HATTY I gather her daughter has done something she shouldn't.

MATTY Which girl is that, I wonder? Do you know?

HATTY I think she's called Susan and she stands on the extreme right end of the fifth row back, at assembly every morning. She sang a solo verse in the hymn, at the end of last term.

MATTY What, that pretty child with curly black hair? Fancy that. She doesn't get her looks from her mother.

(MRS. EMMETT *rises, in boredom, and walks round the room, looking at the timetable on back wall.*)

HATTY *(peering at her)* Did you notice how short her skirt is?

MATTY Indeed I did. It's even worse when she sits down. And I don't think she's wearing a petticoat!

(MRS. EMMETT *wanders over towards them and stands in front of them, quite close, looking discontentedly out of window R.*)

Ugh! She reeks of scent.

HATTY It's very vulgar to smell of anything except eau de Cologne, lavender water or carbolic soap!

(MRS. EMMETT *sighs, looks at watch, goes and examines* MISS ROWE's *papers which lie on the table with her spectacle case, fountain pen, etc.*)

MATTY You'd think she'd know better than to read somebody's papers.

(MRS. EMMETT *picks up fountain pen, opens it and admires it.* HATTY *gasps.*)

HATTY The woman has a most colossal nerve. It will be interesting to see how Miss Rowe deals with her.

MATTY Yes. If she tries to bully this one, like she bullies poor Maudie, she'll find she's bitten off more than she can chew.

HATTY An indelicate metaphor, Matty, but apt—remarkably apt. (MRS. EMMETT *returns to her chair, L. of table, and gets out a cigarette from her bag. She is about to put it to her lips and find her lighter, when* MISS ROWE *enters briskly L.*)

MISS R (*barely touching fingers*) Good morning, Mrs. Emmett, sorry to keep you waiting. (*Crosses to her own chair R.*) I hope you weren't thinking of smoking. It's against our rules, you know.

MRS. E (*after a moment*) Just as you like. (*Puts it away.*)

MISS R It's a shame to lead our girls into unfortunate habits, don't you agree?

MRS. E It depends what you mean by unfortunate. I'd rather smoke than eat, any day, but you wouldn't call eating an unfortunate habit, would you?

(*She laughs complacently.* MISS ROWE *gives a sour smile.*)

MISS R Luckily that is not the subject under discussion.

MRS. E Well, what did you want to see me about, Miss Rowe? I haven't got long. I should be at work right now.

MISS R Ah yes, you go out to work, Mrs. Emmett. I expect you need the money to pay Susie's school fees.

MRS. E Oh no. Susie's Dad pays her school fees. He left us, you know, five years ago, but he pays regularly through the bank. I just go out to work for a bit of company, and to help pay for my cigarettes. Anyway, what's all this leading up to?

MISS R This, Mrs. Emmett. Why does Susie need to earn money at night by singing in a dance band?

MRS. E Oh, she doesn't, Miss Rowe.

MISS R (*outraged*) She does! I have a newspaper photo of her, doing it.

MRS. E But she doesn't earn anything. She only does it for fun.

MISS R Fun!

MRS. E Yes. She needs to get out and meet people after being cooped up in this hen-house all day.

MATTY Hen-house! That's a good one.

MISS R She doesn't need anything of the sort. She needs to have a quiet home life where she can prepare herself for her forthcoming examinations.

MRS. E (*satisfied*) Susie'll pass her exams all right. She works hard before she ever goes to any dance. Have you got any complaints about her work? Didn't she come top of her class last term?

MISS R That is true, but how long can she continue to do so, under the strain of late nights and over-excitement?

MRS. E Susie's tough, like me. We thrive on late nights and excitement.

MISS R What you thrive on is not for me to say——

MATTY I could make a guess!

MISS R ——but it's a very wrong environment for a young impressionable girl, besides exposing her to grave moral danger.

MRS. E Moral danger? You mean, someone might make a pass at her? Look, I'm always there on the dance floor, with my boy friend, and the band leader is my brother, Susie's uncle. What harm can she come to?

MISS R (*breathing hard*) Very well, we will leave the moral issues for the moment.

MRS. E Thank you. Surely a mother knows what's good for her own daughter.

MISS R But she might also consider what's good for her daughter's school!

MRS. E What's it got to do with the school?

MISS R The school's good name could be irretrievably ruined by what your daughter is doing—dressing in vulgar immodest clothing and singing common songs in a place of doubtful repute——

MRS. E (*angry*) Here! You mind what you're saying. She doesn't do anything wrong!

MISS R It may not be wrong for an adult woman of the world. For a girl of fifteen, attending my school, it's wrong, and I'm warning you, Mrs. Emmett, that if it doesn't stop, I shall have to take steps. I shan't like to do it but the good name of my school is paramount.

MRS. E Good name? Pooh! The name of this school stinks! If I had my way, Susie'd go to a modern school and learn something worthwhile, but her father insists on sending her to this dump because his sister came here.

HATTY (to MATTY) There was a girl called Emmett, I remember.

MRS. E It may have been a good school then but not any more. No school has the right to dictate what its pupils do in their spare time, and so long as Susie behaves herself in school hours there's nothing you can do about it.

MISS R (crossing to L. and opening door) I see that it is quite useless to appeal to your better nature. One cannot appeal to something non-existent. Good morning, Mrs. Emmett.

MRS. E Good morning, Miss Rowe. (Pauses as she goes out.) And by the way, Susie is singing at another dance tonight. Can I sell you a ticket? (Laughs and goes out triumphantly.)

HATTY First round to Mrs. Emmett.
(MISS ROWE sits, tensely, D.L. in arm chair, looking very angry.)

MATTY Is it true, Hatty? Can Miss Rowe expel Susie for what she did?

HATTY Gracious no. She'd have to do something much worse than that before Miss Rowe could take steps, as she calls it. Really though, she handled that interview very badly, don't you think? One should never threaten people like that.
(An outburst of whistling comes from off R. MISS ROWE rises and crosses, opens door and speaks sharply through it.)

MISS R Will you kindly stop whistling! My work requires great concentration.
(Whistling stops. She closes door and sits at table, thinking and playing with pen.)

MATTY (surprised) Who's in there?

HATTY The decorators. Didn't you know? They started stripping it down this morning.

MATTY Oh, Hatty! That wallpaper that we had put up the year before we died?

HATTY Yes, it was getting very shabby, you know.

MATTY But it was sweetly pretty. I hope they'll put something nice in its place.

HATTY Hm. Miss Rowe is hardly the type for primroses and bluebells.

MATTY (*mischievously*) What do you think would suit her personality?

HATTY (*after taking a look at* MISS ROWE's *unpleasant expression*) Distemper!

MATTY (*after a pause*) When are we going to start haunting, Hatty? You said we'd start today.

HATTY Yes. What do you suggest for a start?

MATTY Well, frighten the woman. Like ghosts do in books and on the pictures.

HATTY Do they? How?

MATTY How?

HATTY Yes. Show me.

MATTY Well—(*Rises.*) They loom up behind people.

HATTY Go on then, loom.

MATTY (*going behind* MISS ROWE) And they lift up their hands and make a hideous face and give a sort of moan. (*She does all these things but* MISS ROWE *is too wrapt in thought to notice.*)

HATTY (*not impressed*) No, no. It's not at all what I had in mind. I'm sure only very ill-bred ghosts behave in such a way.

MATTY (*returning to sit beside* HATTY *again*) Oh dear, I don't really know how well-bred ghosts behave. Except—yes, there was a film once, called 'The Ghost Goes West', do you remember, with Robert Donat as a Scottish ghost. Oh he was adorable in his kilt, and he passed through walls and doors in the most well-bred way imaginable. Do you know, Hatty, I saw that film three times! Wonderful man. Wonderful voice. Even now, when I think of his voice— (*She goes into a day dream.*)

HATTY You're talking like a schoolgirl, Matty. Come back to the subject. What you don't seem to realise is that we are very inexperienced at haunting. I for one am quite incapable of passing through a wall, with or without a kilt.

MATTY Me too. It probably takes years of practice.

HATTY I haven't the time for years of practice. If we are to start today we must learn how to materialise. (*Rises and crosses to L.*)

MATTY (*uncertainly*) Materialise?

HATTY Appear, Hatty, appear! How can you frighten anyone if they can't see or hear you?

MATTY Oh. No, they can't, can they?

HATTY (*crossing again towards* MATTY) I believe it's simply a matter of will power.

MATTY Oh dear, I've never had a lot of will power.

HATTY I have. And before this day's over I shall——
(*She is interrupted by* MAY DANVERS *entering L. carrying register.* HATTY *sits.*)

MAY I'm sorry I had to send for the register again. Sandra Peters turned up at half past nine after I'd marked her absent.

MISS R Yes, yes, leave it here. Please sit down, Miss Danvers, there's something I want to speak to you about. It's a matter which needs very discreet handling.

MAY (*sitting L. of table*) You can always rely on my discretion, Miss Rowe.

MISS R I'm sure I can. In fact, I am giving you my confidence because I think we see eye to eye about a certain girl in this school. I am referring to Susan Emmett. Have you seen the local newspaper?

MAY Oh yes, Miss Rowe, and that dreadful photograph. It's really disgraceful to think of one of our girls behaving in such a way. I was tempted to show it to you myself but I didn't want to get her into trouble——

MISS R Naturally, Miss Danvers, but in matters like this one has to overcome one's kindlier impulses and think first of the honour of the school.

MATTY (*irreverently*) Hooray!

MISS R I have just had an interview with the girl's mother which has been most unsatisfactory. She appears to delight in her daughter's behaviour and its effect on our good name.

MAY How incredible. I mean—the sort of mother who'd let her daughter——

MISS R Precisely. That sort of mother and that sort of daughter are not wanted here.

MAY I've often felt that this was the wrong school for Susan.

MISS R She works well, I believe.

MAY Yes, I must admit I have no complaints about her work.

MISS R So we can't get rid of her on that score.

MAY You mean—?

MISS R To be frank, Miss Danvers, I shan't be happy till I have forced Mrs. Emmett to remove her daughter. Unfortunately, her sudden notoriety as a dance-hall singer is not quite sufficient grounds for me to—do anything.

MAY No, I suppose it isn't really a crime.

MISS R A crime. It's odd you should use the word crime. In a school one often finds an outbreak of petty crime, doesn't one? Last term, for instance, there were several small things stolen, do you remember?

MAY Yes, someone's wrist watch and a manicure set were taken.

MISS R We never found the culprit.

MAY No. You said if anything else were taken you would go to the police. Oh! Do you think it was Susan Emmett?

MISS R I don't know, and it's too late now to find out. But it did occur to me that the pilfering might break out again.

MAY (blankly) It might, I suppose, but it's very difficult to pin the guilt on the right girl.

MISS R Not if the missing articles—something of mine or yours, perhaps—were actually found in the girl's desk, Miss Danvers.

MAY (with a gasp) I think I see what you mean.

MISS R (meaningly, with a long look) I'm sure you see what I mean, Miss Danvers. This pen, for instance has a real gold cap. I sometimes leave it on my desk and anyone could help themselves.

MAY You mean—you want me to——

MISS R (hastily) There's no need to put it into words. But I can promise you that a well carried out scheme would not go unrewarded.

(MAY stares at her silently.)

HATTY Do you realise what these two are plotting to do, Hatty?

MATTY I do. That unfortunate child is going to be framed.

HATTY Not if I can help it. Of all the unscrupulous—

MAY (*making up her mind and rising*) Very well, Miss Rowe. I'll see what I can—arrange.

MISS R Thank you, Miss Danvers. It makes a pleasant change to get a little helpful co-operation from a member of staff. (MAY *smirks*.)

HATTY Wait and see what you get from two ex-members! (*School bell rings, off* L.)

MISS R Ah, break. (*She rises*.) I don't think I'll stay. It gets so crowded when the staff come in. I'll go and see how Pargeter has hung the new picture in the hall.

MAY It looks wonderful, Miss Rowe. I'm sure it will be quite an inspiration to us all at assembly.

MISS R Yes, I think the girls will like it. (*She goes out* L.)

HATTY They'll love it. I found a penknife and frayed the cord nearly through. With a bit of luck it'll fall in the middle of the first hymn.

MATTY Oh, Hatty, you are a devil! (*Admiringly*.)

HATTY No, I'm not. I'm a very fair-minded woman, but in the last few days I have been tried beyond endurance.

(MRS. THORPE *enters* L., *rousing* MAY *from thought*.)

MRS. T (*aggressively*) So that's where you are. Do you realise that your class has been running riot for the last fifteen minutes? I never heard such an uproar.

MAY I had to speak to Miss Rowe.

MRS. T Well, why didn't you set them some work? Janice Avery was walking on her hands up and down the gangway and the others were cheering her on.

MAY (*nastily*) I'm sorry they disturbed you.

MRS. T Well, I was trying to take a poetry lesson about the Lake Isle of Innisfree. (*Quotes with emotion*.) 'And I shall have some peace there, for peace comes dropping slow'. The girls were convulsed. (*Crosses and throws herself heavily on the sofa, narrowly missing the* PYE *sisters who move smartly aside. She pulls off her shoes and massages her feet*.)

HATTY It's going to get a bit crowded in here. Shall we go, before someone sits on us? Not that they'd notice but it would be so undignified from our point of view.

MATTY (*rising*) Let's go and see where they've hung us in the chemistry lab. I hope I'm not opposite that row of bottled intestines. (*Crossing as she speaks. As she opens the door* SALLY *is revealed carrying a tray of steaming cups.*)

SALLY (*entering*) That was funny. I was just going to give the door a good kick when the wind blew it open for me.

MRS. T This staffroom is the draughtiest hole in the school. (SALLY *places tray on table.*)

MATTY (*lingering*) That coffee smells so good.

HATTY Well, it's not for you. (*Drags her out and shuts door.*)

SALLY (*staring*) It's a very obliging draught.
(*They all help themselves to coffee.* MAY *takes hers to easy chair, D.L.,* MRS. THORPE *returns to sofa R.,* SALLY *takes hers over to the telephone table at back.*)

MAY (*after a sip*) Has this got sugar in it?

SALLY Oh, Miss Danvers, I'm so sorry. I put sugar in all of them. I didn't have room on the tray for the sugar bowl.

MAY Ugh. It's too bad. I've told you dozens of times that I hate sugar in coffee.

MRS. T Coffee without sugar tastes like—senna pods!

MAY Your palate has to be educated to the taste.
(*Enter* JANE L.)

MRS. T Oh heavens, let's leave education out of it.

JANE (*going to drink some coffee*) Yes, let's. It's so unnecessary I always think. I've just been struggling to teach the girls that coffee comes in beans from Brazil, when they all know perfectly well that it really comes in tins from Marks and Spencers.

MAY (*to* SALLY *who is taking two cups of coffee towards door U.R.*) Where are you going?

SALLY I thought I'd take a drink in to Pargeter and Son. It's very thirsty work, decorating.

MAY Oh yes? And you're dying to have a close-up of them, I suppose.

SALLY Well, he is rather gorgeous, isn't he?

JANE Who? Pargeter?

SALLY No, Son. Have you seen him?

JANE No. What's he like?

SALLY Like a young Greek god. And painfully shy. I said 'Good

morning' to them and he went absolutely scarlet. It made
his shirt look whiter than white.

MRS. T Spare us the commercial. What's the father like?

SALLY Oh, he's not shy. A bit too up and coming, if you ask me.
Not bad looking, only sort of—capriform! Would you
open the door, please, Miss Cox? Thank you. (*She sweeps
out, leaving the others staring.*)

MRS. T Capriform! Well I never!

MAY That girl gets more and more ridiculous. She's always trying to show off.

JANE I wonder if he minds being capriform?

MRS. T I believe it's quite incurable.

JANE Quick, let's look it up before she gets back. (*Finds dictionary beside telephone, sits at table and searches.*)
Caprice—capricious—capricorn——

MRS. T That's a sign of the Zodiac.

JANE —here it is. Capriform. Having the form of a goat!
(*She shuts dictionary and leans on it as* SALLY *returns,
starry eyed.*)

MRS. T Well, what did the old goat say?

SALLY Oh, you've looked it up. He said I was a sight for sore eyes.

MRS. T Did he, the wretch!

JANE And what did the young one say?

SALLY (*dreamily*) Oh, it was thrilling. He looked down at me from
an enormous height, wiped his hands on his overalls, gave
a funny little smile and said—'Ta, miss'.

MAY (*with a snort of disgust*) 'Ta, miss!'

SALLY Ah, but it's the way he says it. His adam's apple goes up
and down and his eyebrows give a sort of twitch. And
he's got golden hairs all up his arms, and—oh, it's his
shape!

MRS. T This gets more and more enthralling. Tell me about his
shape!

MAY Oh, don't encourage her.

SALLY He's so triangular. You know, wide shoulders and incredibly narrow hips. When he reaches up with his paintbrush,
his stomach just caves in!

MRS. T (*clutching her bosom in ecstasy*) Oh, don't go on. I'm all
weak at the knees.

C

(JANE *is very amused but* MAY *is indignant.*)

MAY You two are disgusting! Honestly, you make me ashamed. And you're the worst, Mrs. Thorpe, a married woman and a mother.

MRS. T Well, I should never have been either of those if I had been insensible to manly beauty. Not that poor, dear Herbert ever really looked like a triangular Greek god.

MAY As for Sally, she can't help being stupid but she might try and behave like a lady. No ex-pupil of this school would look twice at a man of that class.

SALLY (*annoyed*) I'll look as many times as I like——

JANE (*intervening*) Sally, I wonder if you'd be a dear and take some coffee down to Miss Maudesley. She's on playground duty and I know she feels the cold.

SALLY (*forgetting her annoyance*) Yes, of course I will. Poor old Maudie. Just her luck to get playground duty the first week of term.

(*Exit* SALLY L., *carrying coffee cup.* MRS. THORPE *gets her knitting out of a capacious bag that she carries.*)

MRS. T Has anyone seen my spectacles? I seem to have left them somewhere.

MAY Are you sure they haven't been—taken?

MRS. T Taken? You mean, stolen? Why should they? Nobody else could wear them.

MAY No. But they've got rather pretty frames. Some girl has probably taken a fancy to them.

JANE What makes you say that?

MAY Several things were taken last term, weren't they, Mrs. Thorpe?

MRS. T Two things, in fact. (*Starts to knit.*)

MAY Yes, quite valuable things. And I myself have mislaid a purse with two pounds in it.

JANE Really? When did you last have it?

MAY Yesterday afternoon when I was teaching your class. I wanted to show them the black line and the water mark in a pound note. I must have left it on your desk but when I went back at the end of the afternoon it had gone.

JANE I'll enquire very closely into this, Miss Danvers. I don't like to think that any of my class is under suspicion.

MAY (*nastily*) Oh no, of course not. Your girls are all perfect little angels. They might sing lowdown songs in night clubs but they wouldn't steal a farthing.

JANE I thought you'd be bringing that up soon, but kindly remember that it was not a night club and the songs were of the ordinary popular variety.

MAY So that makes the whole thing blameless, does it?

JANE By no means. I had a little talk with Susie myself, before school this morning, and it's quite obvious the child only does it to please her mother and her uncle who is the band leader.

MAY Don't tell me she hates every minute of it. You could see by the photo how she was revelling in it.

JANE Oh yes, she admits it's quite fun, especially dressing up and making people believe she's grown up. I tried to make her see how that could lead her into trouble but—she's so darned innocent that I just couldn't make her understand.

MAY Innocent! She's obviously fooled you very successfully. Luckily Miss Rowe has seen the photo in the paper——

JANE Oh no!

MAY —without my saying a word about it, and she'll know how to deal with it. She's already seen the girl's mother and warned her to watch her step if she wants her daughter to continue at this school.

JANE I honestly believe you'd be delighted if—
(*Enter* SALLY L., *in a hurry.*)

SALLY What do you think! Maudie's in trouble again!

MRS. T Maudie? How? (*Puts down knitting.*)

JANE What do you mean?

SALLY Alderman Pursey's precious daughter Angela has fallen off the climbing frame and sprained her ankle, and Hard Rowe says it was Maudie's fault.

JANE How on earth could Maudie have prevented her from falling? Was she supposed to have caught her?

MRS. T Some hopes. That girl weighs ten stone at least!

SALLY Well, Maudie was on playground duty, and that makes her responsible, you see. It was quite a scene: Angela Pursey bawling and carrying on, and Maudie all white and trembling and Hard Rowe looking grim and saying 'gross inefficiency' and things like that.

JANE How unfair! I bet the girl hasn't really hurt herself.

SALLY Well, she's lying down in the rest room and Miss Rowe is applying a cold compress with her own fair hands because Alderman Pursey mustn't be offended whatever happens. (*Bell rings.*)

MRS. T Heavens, the bell! Who am I taking? Jane, look at the time-table for me! (*Hurriedly packs away her knitting.*)

JANE (*consulting timetable*) Upper Fourth, Grammar.

MRS. T Crikey! I thought that was tomorrow.
(*JANE seizes books from table.*)

MAY Those are my books you're taking.

JANE (*putting them down*) Sorry. Where are mine? (*Goes down on knees beside cupboard D.L.*) These are all yours, Thorpey. What a mess! Oh, here are mine, underneath.

MRS. T Don't flap, dear. The girls aren't any more eager to start than we are.

MAY (*going out*) Speak for yourself, Mrs. Thorpe. (*Exit L.*)
(*MRS. THORPE and JANE sort out their books on floor.*)

JANE Do you think May Danvers is a good teacher?

MRS. T Well, the girls don't like her but she gets good results. (*They start to go,* JANE *first.*) With me, it's the other way about. The girls just love me and the results are frightful. (*Exit* JANE *and* MRS. THORPE. SALLY *collects all the coffee cups and puts them on tray on table. Then she goes to enter the room U.R., but at the last moment stops, gets out compact from her pocket, powders her nose, smiles and puts away compact, then goes and opens door R.*)

SALLY Have you finished your coffee? (*She goes out, closing door smartly.*)
(*Almost at once* HATTY *and* MATTY *enter L.* HATTY *is obviously put out and marches indignantly across the stage, thumping a little with her stick.*)

HATTY It's perfectly ridiculous to blame Miss Maudesley. I saw the whole thing from the laboratory window, didn't you?

MATTY (*investigating empty coffee cups*) No dear. I wasn't looking.

(She drinks the dregs of several cups with obvious pleasure.)

HATTY That fat child, who looks every bit as unpleasant as her father used to, was on the climbing frame behaving in a most stupid and dangerous fashion. Maudie warned her once, and as soon as Maudie's back was turned she made a rude face and did the same trick again. I was quite gratified when she fell off but the way that Rowe person bullied poor Maudie was quite unforgivable. The poor dear looked as if she was going to faint.

(Door opens U.R. and SALLY appears with two cups.)

SALLY *(beaming)* Thank you so much, Mr. Pargeter.

(The door is closed behind her. She puts cups on tray, picks up tray, approaches D.L., finds it closed, sighs and takes tray back to table.)

MATTY I'll open it for you, dear.

(She opens it. SALLY turns, empty handed, and is amazed to find it open.)

SALLY How uncanny.

(Exit SALLY with tray of cups. After a moment, MATTY closes door behind her.)

MATTY A nice girl, that.

HATTY Give me your attention, Matty. Things have gone far enough.

MATTY Are we going to start haunting, Hatty?

HATTY Yes. Somehow we have got to get through to Maudie and give her some advice and some help. To do that, we must appear. It will frighten her a bit—but——

MATTY It frightens me a lot!

HATTY Nevertheless it must be done.

MATTY I don't know how to.

HATTY Remember one of father's favourite sayings, 'Head straight into the wind'.

MATTY Yes, dear. Which way is it blowing?

HATTY No, no. Come and stand here beside me.

(MATTY does so. They face the audience.)

Now I want you to take a deep breath, shut your eyes and say to yourself, 'I *will* appear, I *will*.'

MATTY Yes, Hatty. Now?

HATTY Yes. Now.

(They shut their eyes, breathe deeply, and their lips move. Their faces show fierce concentration. After a moment, MISS MAUDESLEY *enters L. She is startled at seeing a stranger.)*

MAUDIE Oh, I beg your pardon. Were you wanting to see the head-mistress?

HATTY *(very kindly, crossing to her)* No dear. It's you I've come to see.

MAUDIE Me? But I don't think I— *(She falters, staring.)* Do I know you? You remind me so much of—someone.

HATTY *(leading her to easy chair D.L., and drawing up a chair for herself while* MATTY *hovers anxiously behind her)* I know I do, dear. Someone you knew, years ago. Someone who was once headmistress here.

MAUDIE *(trembling)* Miss Harriet.

HATTY Yes, dear. I am Miss Harriet.

MAUDIE But I thought you were dead.

HATTY I am, dear. Please don't be frightened. I want to help you. That's why I'm here.

MAUDIE *(accepting the situation)* You're a ghost.

HATTY Yes. You mustn't be afraid of me.

MAUDIE I'm not. I always thought if I saw a ghost I'd die of fright —but when it's you—oh, I'm so glad to see you, Miss Harriet. And dear Miss Matilda, where is she?
*(*MATTY's *face falls.)*

MATTY Hatty, she can't see me. I haven't appeared.

HATTY She's here with me, Maudie. Can't you see her?

MAUDIE No.

HATTY Bad luck, Matty. You'll have to practise some more.

MATTY It's no good. I haven't enough will power. Oh, I am disappointed. *(Goes and sits on sofa R.)*

MAUDIE Is she really there? Dear Miss Matty. I've missed you so much. Things were so different when you and your sister were alive. I was happy teaching here, then. Now I feel as if—*(Half in tears.)*—I can't go on.

HATTY We're here to help you, Maudie, if we can. And we saw what happened when that naughty child fell off the climbing frame. You were not to blame.

MAUDIE Miss Rowe says it was 'culpable negligence'. She says I'm

to spend my free period writing a letter of apology to
Alderman Pursey.

MATTY Oh, the very idea!

HATTY You'll do nothing of the sort. Now, Maudie, you're a dear
sweet soul but you must have more courage. More back-
bone. Stand up for yourself.

MAUDIE But I'm so afraid of losing my job.

HATTY Nonsense. You're an excellent History teacher and Miss
Rowe knows it. She's very lucky to have you and if you
left she'd have great difficulty replacing you. Show her
that you know it. Threaten to leave!

MAUDIE Oh, I couldn't.

HATTY (to MATTY) How can I get her to fight back?

MATTY Poor dear, it isn't in her nature and it never was. She's fair
game for any bully that comes along.

HATTY Maudie, how long before you can afford to retire?

MAUDIE I'll have paid off the house in another three years. It would
have been paid off before, only Mother had to have an
operation and she just won't go on the National Health,
so there didn't seem——

HATTY Three years! Are you prepared to be bullied and brow-
beaten for another three years just because you haven't
the courage to——

MATTY Hatty dear, who's bullying now?

HATTY (rising) Yes, you're right. It doesn't help to shout at the
poor dear. I'll have to think of something else.

MATTY If only Maudie could do something very special that would
make Miss Rowe appreciate her.

HATTY (toying with the idea) Yes—there's the germ of an idea
there. Something special. Something to gladden the heart
of a nasty snobbish, unscrupulous character like Miss
Rowe. I wonder——

MATTY (in a panic) Someone's coming!

MAUDIE It's Miss Rowe. Quick, you mustn't let her catch you here.
(Rises.)

MATTY Disappear, Hatty! Hurry up! Concentrate! Oh, Hatty,
what's the matter? Can't you do it?
(During these speeches HATTY remains very calm and
thoughtful, looking at the door, behind which we can

hear MISS ROWE *telling* SALLY, *'Be sure and let me know as soon as the car arrives to take Angela home.' Enter* MISS ROWE L. *She pauses in the doorway and stares haughtily at* MISS HATTY, *who returns her gaze unmoved.*)

MATTY That's torn it.

MISS R I was not aware that we had a visitor. Is this a friend of yours, Miss Maudesley?

MAUDIE Yes, Miss Rowe. She arrived rather unexpectedly——

MISS R (*freezingly*) I hope you informed your friend that we do not entertain on the school premises. This is a school, not a social club.

MAUDIE Yes, Miss Rowe. She's just going——

HATTY (*imperiously*) Allow me to introduce myself. I am the Grand Duchess Anna of Schneswig-Hüfstein. You must be Miss Rowe, the Headmistress, yes?

MISS R (*automatically accepting her extended hand*) The Grand Duchess Anna?

HATTY (*developing a German accent*) Of Schneswig-Hüfstein. You have, of course, heard of our little country which has been so much in the news lately.

MISS R (*still suffering from lack of poise*) Er—yes, of course. But I had no idea that our Miss Maudesley had any—connections, with your country.

HATTY Connections? Indeed she has. Maudie is my very dear friend. Have you never spoken of me to your Headmistress, Maudie?

MAUDIE Well, no. I don't believe I have.

HATTY Ah, you are so reserved, you English. Yes, we have been friends since childhood, Maudie and I. You know, of course, that she is distantly related to the Royal Family of Schneswig-Hüfstein?

MISS R Indeed I did not.

HATTY Dear Maudie, so incredibly modest. It is only a distant connection, of course, but both she and I can trace our ancestry back to Prince Wolfgang the Terrible. Have you taught the girls about Wolfgang the Terrible and his amazing effect on the history of Schneswig-Hüfstein, Maudie?

MAUDIE Er—not yet, Anna.

HATTY   Perhaps you are wise. His way of life was rather—unconventional. Young girls might find the details too exciting.

MISS R   Won't you sit down, Your Highness?

HATTY   (*seating herself in armchair L., with royal composure*) That is most kind of you.

MISS R   Not at all. We are deeply honoured by your visit. Miss Maudesley, do sit down, my dear. You must be tired after doing playground duty.
(*As* MAUDIE *chooses a chair C., and sits down,* MATTY *leans forward agitatedly.*)

MATTY   Hatty, are you quite mad?

HATTY   No. I know what I'm doing.

MISS R   I beg your pardon, Your Highness?

HATTY   I—know I am doing the right thing in coming here personally to look at your school.

MISS R   Surely you haven't come all the way from Schneswig Hapstein——

HATTY   Hüfstein.

MISS R   Hüfstein, just to look at our school?

HATTY   Indeed I have. How else could I be sure if it would suit Brunhilde?

MISS R   Brunhilde?

HATTY   Maudie, dear, surely you have told them about Brunhilde?

MAUDIE   (*helplessly*) No, Anna. I haven't told them about anything.

HATTY   The Crown Princess Brunhilde is my niece. She is thirteen years old. A dear girl, very shy and retiring. Being born many years later than her seven brothers, she has led a rather lonely life at the Palace, and has no companions of her own age and sex. I'm sure you will agree that such a life is not good for a young girl.

MISS R   I do agree.

HATTY   At last, after constantly refusing to take my advice, my brother, the Archduke Ludwig, decided she must go to school. By a strange coincidence, that very same day I received a letter from Maudie. She spoke in such glowing terms of Gibraltar School that I showed the letter to Ludwig and he said to me, 'Anna, you must go and inspect this school because it might be the very place for Brunhilde.'

MISS R *(in delight and amazement)* This is extremely gratifying. Do please inspect the school and if there is any little thing wrong, don't hesitate to mention it.

HATTY *(rising and crossing towards* MATTY *and gazing out of window)* Anything wrong?

MATTY *(sharply)* There's a lot of things wrong. In the first place I don't believe an Archduke's daughter can be a Crown Princess.

HATTY Oh, that's awkward.

MISS R What is awkward, Your Highness?

HATTY It's awkward to find any fault with dear Maudie's school. In her letter she described the happy atmosphere, the warm sympathy of the Headmistress, the sensible way in which the girls are treated—no preference given to girls with rich or influential parents.

(MISS ROWE *looks guilty.*)

That is how we would want it for Brunhilde. No preferential treatment. Yes, I have to look into the practical side, for my brother Ludwig is a romantic.

MISS R Really? In what way is he a romantic?

HATTY You will laugh when I tell you. He has fallen in love with the name of your school. Is it not ridiculous? The Crown Prince Ludwig of Schneswig-Hüfstein, in love with that quaint name, Gibraltar School.

MAUDIE Oh, but Miss Rowe and the governors have decided to change——

MISS R *(interrupting)* No, Miss Maudesley, you are mistaken. There was a suggestion of a change of names but I firmly vetoed the idea. Have no fear, Your Highness, that quaint old name shall not be changed while I am in charge.

HATTY I see you are a romantic too.

MATTY Like heck she is!

(HATTY *turns angrily and silently admonishes her for such vulgarity. Enter* SALLY, *without knocking.*)

SALLY Oh! *(Hesitates.)* I'm sorry to interrupt you, Miss Rowe, but you wanted to know when the car came for Angela.

MISS R Oh yes, I was going to— *(Changes her mind.)* No. You can help her in, Sally. There's no need for anyone to go with her.

SALLY No need? Oh, I'm sorry. I understood that you were going home with her to speak to Alderman Pursey.

MISS R Certainly not. Angela must not expect preferential treatment, just because her father is an Alderman.

(SALLY *gapes at this sentiment*.)

HATTY Splendid.

MAUDIE I'm afraid I haven't written that apology yet, Miss Rowe.

MISS R Then don't, Miss Maudesley. You were in no way to blame for Angela's silliness. Help her into the car, Sally, and tell her she is forbidden to use the climbing frame for the rest of the term.

(SALLY *goes out, round-eyed*.)

HATTY How glad I am to see you support your teachers so firmly. It is so bad for discipline if the girls sense that you are at odds with the staff.

MISS R Of course, Your Highness. How well you understand.

HATTY This girl's father. You say he is Alderman? Is that some rank of nobility? Some kind of lord, perhaps?

MISS R Gracious no. He's quite an ordinary man, but a member of the town council. However, he's a very rich man and generous towards our school. Only this term he has donated a splendid modern painting, which we have hung in the Assembly Hall. It cost him two hundred pounds.

HATTY How praiseworthy! I would love to see it. I adore modern paintings.

MATTY You hypocrite.

MISS R I shall be very happy to show it to you. It is most impressive.

HATTY Obviously you do not neglect to surround your girls with lovely things. Tell me, who is the painter of this masterpiece?

MISS R His name is Korginsky, I believe. You may have heard of him. Vladimir Korginsky.

(HATTY *halts and stiffens at the first mention of the name*.)

HATTY (*slowly, in a whisper*) Did you say Vladimir Korginsky?

MISS R Yes. Have you heard of him?

HATTY (*dramatically, as if to herself*) Vladimir Korginsky! Oh, am I never to be rid of you? Must your shadow always cast its darkness over our family?

MISS R   Your Highness, you distress me. Who is this man?

HATTY   (*still to herself*) Of course. Even then he was making a name for himself as a painter.

MISS R   Even then?

HATTY   Vladimir Korginsky was the son of a steward at our winter palace. He was the same age as Crown Prince Bruno. They became great friends. Poor Bruno, so full of promise, so clever and talented. We little guessed what dens of vice that villain would lead him into.

MISS R   Dens of vice?

HATTY   Dope, Miss Rowe. Vladimir Korginsky turned the Crownprince of Schneswig-Hüfstein into a drug addict!

MISS R   How appalling!

HATTY   (*with great emotion*) My favourite nephew, the handsomest of the seven, so strong and brave and good, is now a gibbering lunatic in an asylum. And you ask me to admire the work of the man responsible? No, Miss Rowe, I will not see it, and neither shall the Crown Princess Brunhilde. Some other school shall have her. Not this one, where the devil incarnate exhibits his wicked talents. (*Very dramatically spoken.*)

MATTY   (*clapping*) Well done, Dame Sybil Thorndike!

(HATTY *bows in her direction and prepares to sweep out.*)

MISS R   (*slipping anxiously across to intercept her*) No, please wait a moment, Your Highness. Naturally I had no idea of the man's history. I'll have it taken down at once.

HATTY   And incur the wrath of your Alderman?

MISS R   But he doesn't know the truth. When I tell him the artist is a dope addict——

HATTY   (*sternly*) Miss Rowe, I advise you to say nothing of that to anyone. You will do your school no good if you become involved in a slander suit.

MISS R   You think that man would dare—?

HATTY   Vladimir Korginsky would dare anything. And remember, the greater the truth, the greater the libel. No, no, it is better that you should hang your picture and say nothing. The Princess Brunhilde must find another school.

MISS R   (*desperately*) Your Highness, I beg you not to say that. The picture shall not be hung. I shall arrange for—an—accident to happen to it.

HATTY (*looking at her thoughtfully*) Miss Rowe, you are a woman of determination. What is more, you appear to have the courage of your convictions.

MISS R Well, I can assure you that once I make up my mind about something, I allow nothing to stand in my way.

HATTY I too, have something ruthless in my character. I wonder if I should have made a good headmistress?

MISS R (*smiling*) Oh no, your Highness, you come from a different world.

MATTY How right you are.

MISS R Now, may I have the honour of showing you over the school?

MATTY Oh, Hatty, all those stairs! And your arthritis!

HATTY Of course, Miss Rowe. Whether or not the Princess Brunhilde comes here may well depend on what I see. Are you coming too, Maudie?

MAUDIE I'm afraid I can't. I have to take a P.E. class in a few minutes.

HATTY P.E.? What is that?

MAUDIE Physical Education.

HATTY (*amazed*) Physical Education? You mean gymnastics? At your age?

MISS R (*hastily*) Miss Maudesley is so enthusiastic, one tends to forget she is not so young as the rest. I did suggest that it might be too much for her, but she insisted, didn't you, Miss Maudesley?

MAUDIE (*unhappily*) Well, yes——

HATTY (*vehemently*) Maudie, you are a naughty old woman to insist. You must leave the gymnastic lessons to young teachers. Miss Rowe can easily re-arrange the timetable, can't you, Miss Rowe?

MISS R Of course I can. Miss Cox will gladly do extra P.E. and Miss Maudesley can take Miss Cox's English twice a week.

HATTY There you are, you see. How easy it is when the headmistress is so sympathetic. Now, no more silliness, Maudie, or you'll make yourself ill and then Miss Rowe would be without the best History teacher she has ever had.

MISS R Yes, indeed. No one can teach History like Miss Maudesley.

MAUDIE (*overcome*) You're very kind.

MISS R Just this once the girls can do silent reading. Shall we go, Your Highness? (*She goes to door and opens it.*)

MATTY (*rising*) This I must see. Try and make her shift us back from the stinks lab, Hatty. She's in the mood to do anything you suggest.

HATTY Very well, but don't get in the way. (*She recollects herself and repeats the words to* MAUDIE.) Don't get in the way of doing too much. Cousin Ludwig would be very distressed.

(*Exit* HATTY *followed by* MISS ROWE.)

MATTY That's right, Maudie. And you know what Cousin Ludwig's like when he's distressed.

(*Exit* MATTY. MAUDIE *sits in chair D.L., as if her legs won't hold her any longer. School bell rings.*)

MAUDIE (*whispering*) Cousin Ludwig Princess Brunhilde.

(*Enter* MISS DANVERS.)

MAY (*looking down at* MAUDIE) Having a nice rest?

MAUDIE (*with a start*) Oh. Yes, thank you.

MAY Well? Isn't it time you were getting ready for P.E.?

MAUDIE I'm not taking P.E. this period. Miss Rowe says the girls can do silent reading instead.

MAY (*with scorn*) Silent reading. That'll be a thrill. Honestly, Maudie, that's the lowest depths of incompetence a teacher can sink to, in my opinion.

MAUDIE (*rising and speaking with sudden force*) Thank you for giving me the benefit of your opinion, Miss Danvers. If it's any business of yours I had already decided to give Form Five an extra History lesson—on the reign of Wolfgang the Terrible! (*She goes out.*)

CURTAIN

ACT III

Next day, after school. MRS. THORPE *is on her knees, sorting a pile of lurid paintings in black and white, some of which she props up against the furniture to view them better. Enter* SALLY *with an armful of registers.*

SALLY Whatever are you doing, Mrs. Thorpe?

MRS. T Sorting through the Lower Fifth paintings.

SALLY What are they meant to be?

MRS. T The subject was, 'Ghosts', a study in black and white.

SALLY (*picking up one of them*) I say, this girl's done a lovely skeleton!

MRS. T Yes. Her father's a doctor. Most of them seem to have done flapping white sheets or headless bodies.

SALLY This one's rather unusual.

MRS T Yes. It's obviously supposed to be the Pye sisters, taken from their portraits. Not at all a ghostly picture. I asked her why she did it.

SALLY Who?

MRS. T Susan Emmett.

SALLY What did she say?

MRS T She said that sometimes she gets the feeling that they're still here, keeping an eye on the old school.

SALLY (*shivering*) What a nasty thought.

MRS. T Nasty? I don't think so. But strange—for a girl of her age.

SALLY (*going to her table at rear, to lay down registers*) She was at the dance last night. I hardly recognised her. She was still dancing when I came away at eleven o'clock.

MRS. T Huh! No wonder she's away from school today. Fagged out, I suppose, silly child.

SALLY Young Pargeter was there, too. He danced with Susan several times.

MRS. T Fancy! And how many times did he dance with you?

SALLY Not once. I was bitterly disappointed, but I don't blame him for keeping clear. I was with my brother in full naval officer's uniform. Quite terrifying. (*She is suddenly struck by a thought.*) Mrs. Thorpe!

MRS. T Mm? (*Not looking up.*)

SALLY Young Pargeter hasn't been in today, either. (*They both look at each other for a moment in silence. Then the telephone rings and* SALLY *goes to answer it.* MRS. THORPE *shrugs and goes on sorting pictures, but her expressions show silent comment on* SALLY's *conversation.*)

SALLY (*into telephone*) Gibraltar School. Miss Rowe's secretary here. Oh, Alderman Pursey! (*Her manner is overflowing with charm and helpful sympathy.*) No, I'm afraid Miss Rowe is not here. Can I take a message? Certainly I'll tell her, Mr. Pursey, and I know she's extremely anxious to get in touch with you. She's been trying to find a spare moment all day. And how is poor Angela? Feeling a little better? Oh, I'm so glad. We were all so distressed about her little accident. Nobody's fault, of course, just one of those things—— That's right, Mr. Pursey. Do give her our love and tell her to hurry back. We miss her, you know. Yes, good-bye, sir! (*Rings off.*)

MRS. T (*acidly*) 'Give her our love' indeed! I object to your sending my love to that nasty little brute. Haven't you any conscience about saying things like that? (*Gathers up papers and rises.*)

SALLY Not really. After all, my job depends on keeping old Pursey happy. And I do feel sorry for him.

MRS. T Why? He's got pots of money, a Rolls Royce, a lovely house——

SALLY —and Angela!

(*Enter* MISS ROWE *and* MISS MAUDESLEY.)

MISS R Ah, there you are, Mrs. Thorpe. Are you going home now?

MRS. T Yes, Miss Rowe—unless you want me for something?

MISS R No. I only wanted to know if you could give Miss Maudesley a lift, perhaps. The wind is so cold and I don't like her standing waiting for a bus.

MRS. T Certainly I will. I'd take her every day only she usually stays behind, marking.

MAUDIE Oh, really, it's awfully kind of you. I hope I'm not a nuisance.

MRS. T (*getting coat*) Of course you're not a nuisance. Glad to have company.

MAUDIE (*getting her coat and putting it on*) This wind really seems to go right through you.

MRS. T Yes, the leaves will be off the trees before long. Come on, Maudie, let your thoughts dwell on the prospect of tea. I'm yearning for mine.

MAUDIE (*pausing in doorway*) Thank you, Miss Rowe.

MISS R (*permitting herself a thin smile*) Not at all. Good afternoon, Miss Maudesley.

(*Exit* MRS. THORPE *and* MAUDIE.)

Have you finished that stencil yet, Sally?

SALLY Nearly, Miss Rowe. Only a few more lines.

MISS R Good. You can finish it before you leave.

SALLY (*resignedly*) Yes, Miss Rowe. Alderman Pursey rang up. Wanted to speak to you.

MISS R Oh, he'll have to wait.

(*Enter* MAY DANVERS *and* JANE COX. *They put their books in lockers* D.L. MISS ROWE *is hunting among books and pencils on the table.*)

Has anyone seen my fountain pen?

SALLY (*who has been typing her stencil*) No, Miss Rowe. You usually leave it on the table.

MISS R Yes. Perhaps it is foolish of me to leave a valuable pen lying around.

MAY When did you have it last?

MISS R I don't remember. Yesterday, I suppose.

JANE Is it very valuable?

MISS R Indeed it is. The cap is of pure gold.

MAY Has it a black band and a black holder?

MISS R Yes. Why, have you seen it?

MAY I've seen something very like it. In Susan Emmett's desk.

JANE Susan Emmett again! I don't believe it! And why were you looking in her desk?

MAY The girl happens to be absent and I needed her exercise book.

JANE Well, it's probably her own pen.

D

MAY With a pure gold cap? Most unlikely.

JANE It could be a cheap metal one, that looked like gold at first glance.

MISS R Well, there's one certain way to find out. We'll go and see.

JANE Very well. I shall come too.

MISS R Yes, do, Miss Cox. Since you have such faith in this girl, nothing will convince you but the evidence of your own eyes. Come along Miss Danvers.

(*Exit* MISS ROWE, MAY *and* JANE L. SALLY *looks perplexed and worried. She hunts briefly under pile of books, shrugs and returns to her typing. When her back is turned the door opens U.R., and* MISS MATTY *peeps round.*)

MATTY All right, Hatty, now's our chance.

(*The sisters enter quickly and close door quietly.*)

HATTY Thank goodness. That man Pargeter smokes something foul in his pipe.

MATTY I was coughing so much I could hardly hear what was going on in here.

HATTY This furtive peering round doors is most undignified. As soon as possible we must learn to pass through them.

MATTY Yes, I've tried repeatedly but it's just like banging my head against a brick wall. Can ghosts have concussion, Hatty?

HATTY It seems quite possible, dear. After all, I still suffer with my arthritis. Now quickly, get that fountain pen.

MATTY (*taking it from her reticule*) Here it is. It's rather splendid, isn't it?

HATTY Far too splendid to leave lying around. It's a positive temptation.

MATTY What a lucky thing you saw Miss Danvers putting it in the girl's desk.

HATTY Yes, I wish I could see her face when she finds it gone. Miss Rowe will be very severe with her.

MATTY Miss Rowe will wipe the floor with her, and serve her right, the nasty creature, sneaking round and putting stolen property in innocent girls' desks. Let's put the pen in her locker, Hatty, shall we?

HATTY No. Put it on the table. I want it found as soon as possible, so that the child is cleared of blame.

(MATTY *does so. A sudden hammering noise, off* R., *startles them and* SALLY.)
Whatever is Pargeter doing now?

MATTY Working off his frustration, I imagine. I heard him telling Sally that the Snow Queen gives him the pip!
(MATTY *crosses* L.)

HATTY He has my deepest sympathy.

MATTY (*discovering pile of paintings on cupboard,* L.) Oh, look Hatty! A picture of us!

HATTY (*crossing*) Of us? Are you sure?

MATTY Of course it's us. It's you to the life, with the way you pull your chin in and purse up your mouth. But I'm sure I'm not that fat!

HATTY Oh yes you are—if not fatter!

MATTY Thank you very much. Oh look, it's by Susan Emmett. Do you think she's seen us?

HATTY No. But I think she may be aware of us. Perhaps it would be wise not to appear again if it can be avoided.

MATTY Not even as the Grand Duchess Anna?

HATTY No. I told Miss Rowe I was flying back to Schneswig-Hüfstein today.

MATTY Hatty, I'm a bit worried about the Grand Duchess.

HATTY Why?

MATTY Well, dear, she was a wonderful invention on the spur of the moment and she caused Miss Rowe to change all kinds of disagreeable things—and made her honey-sweet to dear old Maudie ever since—but you see, well—she isn't true—

HATTY Of course she isn't true. But doesn't the end justify the means?
(SALLY *gets up and hunts through the dictionary for some word, and promptly gets absorbed in it.*)

MATTY What I mean is—Princess Brunhilde isn't true either, so how can she ever come to school here? And if she turns out to be false, poor Maudie's life will be unbearable and we shall have made things worse instead of better.

HATTY (*crossing and sitting on sofa* R.) Oh, I think I can handle it. I shall have to write to Miss Rowe—where can I get hold of some crested note paper?—and tell her with regret that the Princess Brunhilde has gone into a convent, but at the same time I will promise her some other royal child who's not quite old enough to leave home, but who'll be coming to Gibraltar School in a few years' time.

MATTY *(going to join her on the sofa)* And that will keep her sweet until after Maudie retires and then it won't matter any more.

HATTY Precisely.

(Enter MISS ROWE, MAY and JANE. All three are very angry.)

JANE Well, I think you ought to apologise.

MAY I'll do nothing of the sort. The pen was there, I tell you.

JANE Well, it isn't there now. And I for one don't believe it ever was.

MAY I don't suffer from optical illusions. At four o'clock the pen was in Susan Emmett's desk.

JANE And at four-thirty it's not. I shouldn't be surprised if you thought I'd taken it.

MAY It's just the sort of thing you would do, to protect Susan.

JANE Oh! Well, if that's the way you feel, why don't we go back and search my desk?

MISS R Calm yourself, Miss Cox.

JANE But I insist! And my locker, to start with. And here's my handbag. *(Picking it up from on top of locker.)* Search that, too!

MISS R Miss Cox! Nobody suspects you, so please be quiet. The whole affair has been most regrettable.

JANE It certainly has. I must warn my girls in future not to buy pens that look like the headmistress's.

MISS R Please don't be sarcastic. I would be glad if you and Sally would go home now. I want a few words with Miss Danvers.

MATTY I'm looking forward to that.

(SALLY and JANE go and get their coats from cupboard.)

HATTY Surely they'll see the pen in a moment.

MATTY They're too excited to see straight.

JANE I have some books to mark before I go. I'll do them in the class room. *(Exit JANE.)*

SALLY *(laying her stencil on top of pen)* I've finished the stencil, Miss Rowe.

MISS R Thank you, Sally. Good afternoon. *(Exit SALLY.)*

MATTY She's covered up the pen. Now what do we do?

HATTY Nothing. Listen.

MISS R (*turning to* MAY, *ominously*) Well, Miss Danvers?

MAY (*desperately*) Miss Rowe, I can't understand it. I put the pen there myself, straight after school. Somebody else must have stolen it.

MISS R Either that, or you stupidly put it in the wrong desk.

MAY Oh no, I'm sure it was Susie's desk.

MISS R In any case, why choose the one day of the week when Susan's away from school? Now, whoever has it, it can't be Susan. Oh, I've no patience with such bungling.

MAY Perhaps we could try again with something else.

MISS R Try again! Small chance of that with Miss Cox watching over the girl like a tigress. Frankly, Miss Danvers, I'm furious. Not only have I lost a valuable pen, but I've lost my only chance of getting rid of Susan Emmett.

MAY I'm sorry, but really, Miss Rowe, I don't see that it's my fault.

MISS R Then you'd better go away and think about it. I don't wish to discuss it with you any more.

(MAY *gets her coat in silence. She pauses at the door L., starts to say something self-righteous, changes her mind and goes out, banging door.*)

MATTY (*with satisfaction*) That sent her off with a flea in her ear.

HATTY (*amused*) Really, Matilda, your language grows more and more picturesque. However, things have turned out very nicely and I think that as soon as our portraits are hung in the Assembly Hall again—

MATTY Oh, have you arranged it?

HATTY The Grand Duchess took such a fancy to them. As I was saying, things will all be settled satisfactorily and we'll be able to give up haunting.

MATTY (*disappointed*) Oh, what a pity. I've so enjoyed having a finger in the pie. You know—meddling——

HATTY Yes, I know. It has been gratifying. But no doubt some opportunity will arise again in the future, when our intervention will be needed. In the meantime, enjoy your last little chance of meddling. Get that pen from under those papers and have it discovered.

MATTY Right ho. Just wait till her back's turned.
(*Noise of hammering breaks out again.*)
Good old Pargeter. That'll fetch her.
(MISS ROWE, *who has been sunk in grim thought in her chair, rises and goes to door R. MATTY avoids her and circles round the table, towards the stencil.*)

MISS R (*at open door*) Mr. Pargeter! Do you mind?
(*With a swift movement, MATTY whips off the papers and in doing so knocks the pen to the floor.*)

MATTY (*in dismay*) Hatty! I've knocked it on to the floor!

HATTY Well, pick it up then. Hurry!

MISS R I believe you are a painter, not a coal miner. If this noise is inevitable, kindly save it for ten minutes, when I shall have gone home. Then you can make all the noise you like and nobody will hear you. (*Closes door.*)

MATTY (*who has been searching*) I can't see it, Hatty.

HATTY Well, you'd better get down on your knees, Matty. I can't, I'm afraid. My arthritis won't let me.

MATTY Oh dear. (*Gets down on knees.*) I didn't see which way it rolled.
(MISS ROWE *crosses briskly to table and sits. She narrowly misses MATTY, crawling across her path. MISS ROWE picks up stencil and looks through it for mistakes.*)

HATTY (*crossly*) There! If we'd only left it under the stencil she would have found it by now. Hurry up, Matty. I'm anxious for her to have it before she goes home or some other child may be suspected.

MATTY (*peering out from under the table*) It's all very well, saying hurry up. The wretched thing is invisible against this carpet.

HATTY (*pointing*) What's that across there?

MATTY (*emerging*) Where?

HATTY Under that cupboard.
(MATTY *crawls across. As she doubles up to peer under cupboard, the door is thrown roughly open and she is precipitated against the cupboard. MRS. EMMETT stands in the doorway, looking distraught and on the verge of tears. MATTY sits dazedly on the floor.*)

MRS. E Miss Rowe!

MISS R *(indignantly)* Mrs. Emmett! This is no way to come bursting into——

MRS. E Has she been in? My Susie, has she been in?

MISS R Been in? Been in what?

MRS. E In school. Has Susie been in school?

MISS R *(rising)* Mrs. Emmett, you know as well as I do that Susie has been absent all day.

MRS. E *(collapsing into chair by table, with a cry of anguish)* Oh no! It can't be true! Oh, whatever shall I do? Whatever shall I do? *(Loud sobbing.)*

MISS R Stop making that dreadful noise, Mrs. Emmett, and tell me what is the matter. Where is Susan?

MRS. E *(sobbing)* I don't know!

MISS R You don't know?

MRS. E She's not been home all night!
(A shocked silence.)

MISS R Susan did not come home last night? My dear woman, you surely don't mean——

MRS. E I haven't seen her since the dance.

MISS R But didn't she come home with you?

MRS. E No, I went home with Ernie, my boy friend. I thought Susie would be coming in later, but I didn't wait up for her. I went to bed. I never meant to go to sleep though. I was going to stay awake till I heard her come in, but I just went out like a light.

MISS R But this morning, when you found she hadn't come home?

MRS. E I thought she'd gone over to sleep at my brother's place. She often does that if she's missed the bus.

MISS R But didn't you ring up your brother?

MRS. E I hadn't got time. I was late for work. You see, I felt sure she'd gone to Bert's so I didn't worry. Then on my way home from work I met Bert and he said he'd not seen her since the hitch-hiker.

MISS R The hitch-hiker?

MRS. E Oh, it's a kind of dance. Well, I just dashed home and she wasn't there, but I was hoping against hope that you'd know where she is.

MISS R My dear woman, I am not omniscient. If you can't keep track of your daughter's movements out of school hours, it's no good turning to me.

MRS. E Oh, you're cruel. I'm so upset, I can hardly think.

MISS R Well, you'd better pull yourself together. Something has got to be done. It's obvious that something has happened to the girl.

MRS. E I know, I know. She's been murdered, or assaulted, or both, and it's all my fault.

MISS R There's no point in letting your imagination run riot.

MRS. E I'm a bad mother, that's what I am. Taking a kid like her to dances like that, and leaving her to come home alone. I'll never do it again. I deserve to be punished. I'm a bad, wicked woman. Her father'll kill me when he finds out.

MISS R Maybe she has gone to her father. Surely that's the obvious solution.

MRS. E No, no. He's at sea. He's a commander of a P & O Liner.

MISS R Hm. Well, she's not with him, then.

MRS. E No, no, she's lying unconscious in some dark alleyway! Some razor gang will have slashed her! She's lying there all bleeding and mutilated——

MISS R (shaking her) Stop it, Mrs. Emmett! Your daughter is in trouble because you chose to ignore my warning, and you let her behave in a brazen and adult fashion which was bound to lead to disaster. I am not at all sorry for you and I don't see why I should be saddled with your problems. However, since you are obviously incapable of doing anything practical, I will ring up the police for you.

MRS. E How can you be so hard! If you'd ever been a mother yourself you'd know how I feel.

MISS R (going to 'phone) If I'd ever been a mother I'd never have got myself into this situation. Hello? Operator? Get me the police station, please. No, I don't know the number. I expect you to know that. Very well, but hurry.
(MATTY crawls out from behind a chair R.)

MATTY Hatty, I think I can see it.

HATTY (not paying attention) What?

MATTY The pen. It's under her feet, I think.

HATTY Well, get it, then; get it!

(MATTY *makes several attempts to get between* MRS. EMMETT'S *feet.* MRS. EMMETT *crosses her legs and nearly kicks* MATTY *in the eye. If in fact, the pen has rolled to some place visible to the audience,* MATTY *can still get entangled with* MRS. EMMETT *before finally realising that the pen is elsewhere.*)

MATTY Oh, really! Did you ever see such heels? She might just as well be on stilts.

MISS R Police? Good. This is Miss Rowe, the headmistress of Gibraltar School. I wish to report a girl missing from her home since last night. The girl's name is Susan Emmett. Her address is— (*She turns enquiringly to* MRS. EMMETT.)

MRS. E Twenty-nine, Ford Street.

MISS R Twenty-nine, Ford Street. Will you send someone to that address to interview the mother as soon as possible. Yes please, and do not send anyone here. I shall not be on the premises.

MATTY I've got it, Hatty. I thought I'd never reach it—

HATTY (*sharply*) Oh, do be quiet, Matty. This is serious.

MISS R There is nothing I can tell you. The girl has not been at school all day. If you have not found her by tomorrow morning, you may contact me here, after nine o'clock. (*She replaces receiver.*)

(MATTY *meanwhile has risen and put pen on table.*)

MATTY (*sitting by* HATTY *on sofa*) Have I missed something? I hit my head and it feels a bit muzzy. Has Susan run away with a hitch-hiker?

HATTY She's disappeared. I don't like the sound of it.

MISS R Now, Mrs. Emmett, the best thing you can do is to get home as soon as possible and when the police come, try and tell them your story coherently, without any hysterics about mutilated bodies.

MRS. E (*more soberly*) Yes, Miss Rowe. I'll go straight home. I wish I didn't feel so trembly.

MISS R I'm afraid there's nothing I can do about that. I am not free at the moment to give you a lift.

MRS. E Don't worry. I think Bert is coming to pick me up in his van. I told him I was coming here.

(*Enter* JANE COX L.)

JANE Excuse me, Miss Rowe. There's someone waiting downstairs for Mrs. Emmett.

MRS. E Oh, that'll be Bert. He's been quicker than I thought. He's very upset. (*Exit* L.)

JANE Poor woman.

MISS R Poor woman, indeed! Your sympathy is misplaced with her, Miss Cox. If ever a woman made a rod for her own back, she did. I warned her something like this would happen, and now it has. Before morning it will be in all the newspapers and my school will be involved in the grossest form of unpleasantness. Police. Reporters. Photographers. Pictures of the desk where the missing girl sat, the exercise book where the missing girl wrote—

JANE Miss Rowe, aren't you in the least concerned about Susan?

MISS R Well, naturally, I don't wish any harm to the girl. I don't suppose any harm has come to her, really. That sort usually land on their feet. She has probably run off for a gay week end in London and not bothered to let her mother know. It's the sheer thoughtlessness of it that infuriates me, causing all this trouble.

(JANE *stalks across to window and stands looking down.*)

JANE Don't you think you should wait till you know the truth before you accuse the child of thoughtlessness?

MISS R You're very self-righteous this afternoon, Miss Cox. Perhaps you think you know the truth?

JANE Yes.

MISS R I beg your pardon?

JANE Miss Rowe, I wonder if you'd care to look out of the window.

MISS R What on earth for?

JANE In a moment I hope to see Mrs. Emmett come out. I want to see her face.

(MISS ROWE *stares.*)

MATTY What's so special about her face?

HATTY I don't know. Help me up, Matty. I want to have a look at Mrs. Emmett's face myself.

(*They kneel up on the sofa.* JANE, *standing, can see over their heads. Unwillingly,* MISS ROWE *comes across and looks. After a pause they all suddenly react.*)

JANE There she is!

MATTY Who's that with her?

MISS R (*amazed*) There's Susan!

JANE Yes, there's Susan. She's with her mother. It was Susan who was waiting downstairs.

(MISS ROWE *turns sharply away and crosses over to L. The* PYE *sisters sit again.*)

MATTY I saw Mrs. Emmett's face. She was so happy, she was— well—transfigured.

HATTY Yes, that just about describes it. Thank heaven that girl is safe.

MISS R So, Susan Emmett is no longer missing. Perhaps you would be kind enough to explain what has been going on, since you know so much about it.

JANE I only know what Susan told me herself, five minutes ago, when she came in looking for her mother. She was very upset, knowing how worried she must be.

MISS R No doubt. And what was her excuse for all the worry and trouble she has caused?

JANE Until an hour ago, she was locked in a cellar under the Masonic Hall.

MISS R (*sarcastically*) Oh come! That's preposterous!

JANE No, the janitor locked her in by mistake last night and didn't go on duty again until mid-afternoon.

MISS R And you believe this trumped-up nonsense that she's bor-rowed out of a cheap comic?

JANE Yes, I believe it. There's the word of the janitor himself and also David Pargeter.

MISS R What has young Pargeter to do with it?

JANE He was locked in with her.

(*Sensation on the sofa!* MISS ROWE *sinks on to a nearby chair, obviously shaken to the core.*)

MISS R All night?

JANE From midnight last night till three o'clock this afternoon.

MATTY How romantic!

HATTY Don't talk like a fool, Matty. Five hours may be romantic. Fifteen is an ordeal.

MISS R I don't believe it. Janitors don't lock up empty cellars.

JANE It wasn't empty. It had a safe in it with the Masonic Funds. Luckily it also had a few stores so they didn't go hungry. Susan says she'll never fancy potato crisps again.

MISS R How can you be so cheerful? ·

JANE Why not? Susan is safe and sound. Surely that's a cause for cheerfulness?

MISS R If this improbable story turns out to be true, the board of governors will not be cheerful, they will be shocked.

JANE (surprised) Shocked?

MISS R Yes, shocked. It is a shocking story, Miss Cox, a young girl of fifteen and a grown man have spent the night together, have they not?

JANE Good heavens, no! Well—in a way, yes, but not in the way you mean.

MISS R There is only one way.

JANE You honestly believe that two nice young people can't pass an innocent night together?

MISS R (with a sneer) Nice young people? A common paperhanger and the daughter of that slut of a woman?

JANE But you can't be certain of a thing like that. A person is innocent, until he's proved guilty.
(Crosses over to L.)

MISS R Miss Cox, I do not need proof. All I need to ask is—why did they go down to the cellar in the first place?

JANE They saw a cat carrying a baby kitten in its mouth. Like all children, Susan found it irresistible, so they followed it down to the cellar and found a nest of new born kittens in a corner behind a big cupboard. They knelt there watching them for quite a while and then when they tried to leave, they found they were locked in.

MISS R It makes a delightful story. I'm afraid the truth might sound rather more sordid. No, Miss Cox, this unsavoury little incident has made up my mind for me. Susan Emmett must go.

JANE Do you mean—expelled?
(HATTY and MATTY rise in indignation.)

MATTY Oh no, she can't mean that!

HATTY That's unjust!

MISS R Expulsion is an unpleasant word. There will be nothing
        public. She will be told to leave at the end of the week
        and her name will be taken off the register.

JANE   Oh, no, please!

MATTY   Hatty, can't you stop her? Can't you appear?

HATTY   How can I? I'm the Grand Duchess Anna who flew back
        to Schneswig-Hüfstein this morning.

MISS R Please understand, Miss Cox, that I owe it to the rest of
        my pupils to take this unpleasant step. In a schoolful of
        young and innocent girls, one tainted or unsound member
        can infect the whole lot. This thing must be rooted out
        before it can spread. Apart from the young lives already
        in my care, next term we shall have the Crown Princess
        of Schneswig-Hüfstein. The Grand Duchess trusts me to
        guard her morally as well as physically and she knows I
        will take no risks.

MATTY   (towering over her, in a temper) You stupid, self-righteous
        Pharisee!

HATTY   Hush, Matty, what's the use?

MATTY   Well, somebody ought to tell her.

HATTY   Come and sit down. Something tells me that Miss Cox will
        say it for you.
        (They sit again on sofa. JANE's face meanwhile shows her
        anger rising to a pitch when she can no longer control it.)

JANE   (furiously) Poppycock!

MISS R (amazed) I beg your pardon?

JANE   Either you are deceiving yourself or you are the biggest
        hypocrite on God's earth.

HATTY   Splendid, girl; say some more!

MISS R Miss Cox, you forget yourself!

JANE   I don't care. You've been looking for an excuse to get rid
        of Susan, simply because she doesn't measure up to your
        snobbish ideas of what constitutes a nice girl. The fact that
        she's brainy and intelligent and gay and sensitive doesn't
        matter, because she hasn't the right accent and her mother
        goes out to work and they go dancing sometimes instead
        of sitting at home reading the Girls' Own Paper. You tried
        to plant your wretched fountain pen on her, but your
        precious Miss Danvers bungled it. I see she has given it

back again, ready to have another try. (*Points angrily to pen, which* MISS ROWE *picks up and stares at.*)

MISS R Given it back?

JANE But now you think you won't be needing that trick after all, because through no fault of her own, she's been locked in with a man all night and that means she's contaminated! Oh, you make me sick, with your nasty, evil little mind.

MATTY Hear, hear!

JANE And tomorrow morning, you'll stand up in that hall looking Christian and noble and say, 'Let us pray' and read a text from the Bible. Your text should be, 'Judge not, that ye be not judged.'

MISS R Miss Cox, this is insufferable. I shall require your resignation.

JANE And you shall have it. I wouldn't stay another term in this school while you're headmistress. I despise you!

MATTY Oh, well done.

JANE And as well as despising you, I'm sorry for you. I saw your face when Mrs. Emmett and Susan came out of that door together, just now. You saw their arms round each other and their eyes shining with love for each other, and your mean little soul was all twisted with envy. You had no concern for Susan when she was missing and no pity for her poor, frightened, foolish mother. And then, when everything turned out all right, you couldn't forgive her for being so happy so you turned her little adventure into something dirty. And Susan must suffer the shame and disgrace of expulsion, while you hide behind the mask of virtue and talk about owing it to your other pupils. Oh God, if there were any justice on earth, something dreadful ought to happen to you! (*She bursts into tears and rushes out* L.)

MATTY Poor Jane. She's awfully upset.

HATTY Yes, and no wonder. It's an outrage.

MATTY She certainly told that woman a thing or two. I liked that bit about, 'Judge not, that ye be not judged.'

HATTY I'm sorry she's resigned. If that other female resigned I'd jump for joy.

MATTY With your arthritis?

HATTY It does it good to move. (*She rises and glances out of window.*)

There goes Jane. She's just missed the bus, I think.

MATTY Oh, what a shame. But look, some friend is giving her a lift.

HATTY That's good. It's humiliating to be seen weeping on public transport.

MATTY The other one's not weeping, you observe.

HATTY No, she's seething. Just look at her face.

MATTY Bet she'd like to take it out on someone.

HATTY Luckily, there's no one left.

MATTY Yes, there is. You're forgetting old Pargeter, peacefully smoking his pipe in the next room.

HATTY Maybe she has forgotten him, too.

(MISS ROWE *rises abruptly.*)

No, she hasn't. Here she goes.

(MISS ROWE *goes to door* R.)

MATTY Poor old Pargeter. I knew she'd have to vent her wrath on someone.

MISS R (*in ominous tones, at open door*) Mr. Pargeter!

(*She goes out, closing door, smartly.*)

MATTY I don't suppose he even knows where his son spent the night.

HATTY He'll not be in doubt much longer.

MATTY Oh, if only I could pass through the wall. I'd love to watch this.

HATTY Well, there's always the keyhole.

MATTY Shall I?

HATTY Why not? I'll just remove the key.

(*She does so and goes and sits* D.L. *in easy chair, looking strangely at the key:* MATTY *crouches and peers through keyhole.*)

MATTY I can't see very much, except the window. Pargeter seems to have an enormous pile of sandwiches on the window sill. Cheese, I think. And some corned beef, I believe. Oh, there's Pargeter's legs, and one hand all streaked with paint. I can't see Miss Rowe at all but she seems to be doing all the talking. Oh, now I can see Pargeter. He's sitting down on the window ledge and laughing! Honestly,

Hatty, he's laughing like anything. He has a remarkable set of teeth for a man of his age. National Health, I suppose. Oh dear, this is so uncomfortable, I'm getting a crick in the neck. (*Rises.*)

HATTY (*thoughtfully*) Matty, would you say that impulsive actions are always wrong?

MATTY (*bewildered*) I don't know, Hatty. You often tell me that I should think twice before I act.

HATTY I have always tried to guard against acting on impulse. It seems to me a sure way of getting into trouble—and yet—I wonder. This afternoon I did an impulsive thing, and the more I think about it, the wiser it seems.

MATTY What did you do, Hatty?

HATTY I turned this key in the lock.

MATTY (*not immediately grasping the situation*) You turned that key—in this lock? Then—they're locked in?

HATTY Yes, dear. Just like Susan Emmett and David Pargeter.

MATTY Just like Susie—Good heavens, Hatty, you're not going to keep them there all night?

HATTY Don't you think it would be poetic justice?

MATTY (*beginning to laugh*) Oh, yes, yes. Most poetic. The biter bit, as they say. Hoist with her own petard. What is a petard? Sally might know. Oh, Hatty, that's a master stroke.

HATTY You think I am right in doing this?

MATTY Oh yes, indeed. Let her find out what it's like to be locked in. Let her spend a night with a common painter. What a glorious joke!

HATTY (*rising abruptly*) Matty, I am not doing this as a joke. Nor in a spirit of revenge either. It is my earnest hope that some good will come of it.

MATTY You mean, after experiencing what Susie experienced, she'll feel a bit of sympathy and not expel her?

HATTY I mean that such is Miss Rowe's dread of scandal that with any luck she may resign. You see, Matty, I think we can rely on Pargeter not to keep his mouth shut.

MATTY That's true. If he can laugh so much over his son's escapade, he'll positively gloat over his own. (*A rattling noise is heard.*) Watch out, she's trying the door.

(*More rattles, then a pause.*)
She can't believe it's true. Now Pargeter will try and open it.
(*More rattling and creaking.*)

MISS R (*off*) Open this door! Open it at once, whoever you are!

MATTY Who does she think it is, I wonder?

HATTY She'll immediately suspect Jane, of course.

MATTY (*worried*) I don't want Jane to be blamed.
(*Rattling and thumping.*)

MISS R Is that you, Miss Cox? Undo this door and don't be so childish!

MATTY She does think it's Jane.

HATTY Don't worry, Matty. Jane is riding across the town in a friend's car. She has a perfect alibi and can clear herself of all suspicion.
(*Pause.*)
They're very quiet in there. I wonder what she's doing?

MATTY I'll have another peep. (*Kneels by keyhole.*) She's opening the window and looking down. So is Pargeter. He's shaking his head and grinning broadly.

HATTY That man's sense of humour is going to be sorely tried in the next few hours.

MATTY I wonder if she'll order him to shin down the drainpipe.

HATTY I doubt if he'd value her honour more than his neck. It's a thirty foot drop to the concrete yard below.

MATTY And the beauty of it is, that window isn't visible to any passers-by. It only gives on to the small courtyard. Remember what she said to Pargeter? 'You can make as much noise as you like and nobody will hear you.'

MISS R (*thumping noisily on door*) Miss Cox, are you there? I demand that you open this door!

HATTY Hoity toity! She demands, you notice.

MATTY She'll change her tune. Pass me a cushion, Hatty. It's hard on the knees down here.

HATTY (*doing so*) What are they doing?

MATTY (*peering*) They seem to be looking through Pargeter's bag of tools. (*Turns with look of dismay.*) Oh, Hatty, he's got a screw driver. He's going to remove the lock. *Now* what do we do?

E

HATTY (*decisively*) Shoot the bolts!

MATTY The bolts. *Are* there any bolts?

HATTY Yes, two. I'll do the top one.
(MATTY *shoots the bottom one.*)

MATTY What an amazing thing. How long have there been bolts on this door?

HATTY Ever since Gibraltar School first started.

MATTY But why?

HATTY I've often wondered. I know this was once a large house before it became a school. Maybe this was the punishment room. Victorian parents thought nothing of locking up naughty children for hours.

MATTY Or maybe they had a violent lunatic locked away, like Mrs. Rochester in 'Jane Eyre'.

HATTY Listen. What do you hear?

MATTY (*ear to keyhole*) Mr. Pargeter working on the lock. What will he do when he finds it's no use?

HATTY Laugh, I expect, bless him.

MATTY Oh, but—what if he takes the door off its hinges?

HATTY You cannot take a closed door off its hinges. It just won't lift until it's open. (*She sits on sofa and leans back.*) Make yourself comfortable, Matty, because I want you to take first shift on keyhole duty. I'll relieve you when you get tired. (*She puts her feet up.*) I'm going to try and have a nap now, or at least a rest. But one of us must stay awake and alert all the night.

MATTY Why?

HATTY (*sitting bolt upright*) Why? Matilda Pye, have you no sense of moral responsibility? You surely don't imagine I'd let anything *happen* to her, do you?

MATTY (*humbly*) No, dear, of course not.
(*There is a brief silence. Suddenly the door handle falls off, startling* MATTY *considerably. The door is tried again and then thumped angrily*)

MISS R (*off*) Open this door, Miss Cox or whoever it is. You can't leave me shut in here all night with this man! Stop laughing, you wretched creature! Miss Cox, please, I know why you've done this, but I won't try to punish you. Miss Cox, I'll not expel Susan Emmett! I give you my word, I'll never worry her again—only please open this door! Please!

HATTY Have another cushion, Matty. It's going to be a long night. (*The thumping redoubles.*)

CURTAIN

PRODUCTION NOTE

One does not need to be a psychologist to understand these characters. They are very straightforward.

Mrs. Emmett, though common and truculent, should not be actively unpleasant. In the last Act one should feel real sympathy for her, but none at all for Miss Rowe who is totally lacking in warmth or humour. When she smiles, it seems to hurt her.

Sally is important because her light-hearted silliness helps to counter-balance the intensity of the others. The two 'ghost' characters, Hatty and Matty, should avoid ghostly voices or horrifying make-up. Let their faces be paler than the others but their behaviour is ruled entirely by their character; Hatty, forceful, practical, sometimes acid, but always with a twinkle in the eye: Matty, youthful, irreverent and more emotional. It is desirable for them to glide about very silently but it should not appear unnatural.

Since the sisters wear black, an effort should be made to introduce gaiety of colour in others, particularly Sally and Mrs. Emmett. Miss Rowe, Miss Danvers and Miss Cox dress smartly and with taste, Miss Maudesley and Mrs. Thorpe rather shabbily.

The set is bound to be drab (staffrooms usually are), but bright curtains and a travel poster would enliven the neutral walls and ancient cupboards. The carpet should be patterned, so that the fountain pen, when it is dropped in Act III, is difficult to see.

G.R.

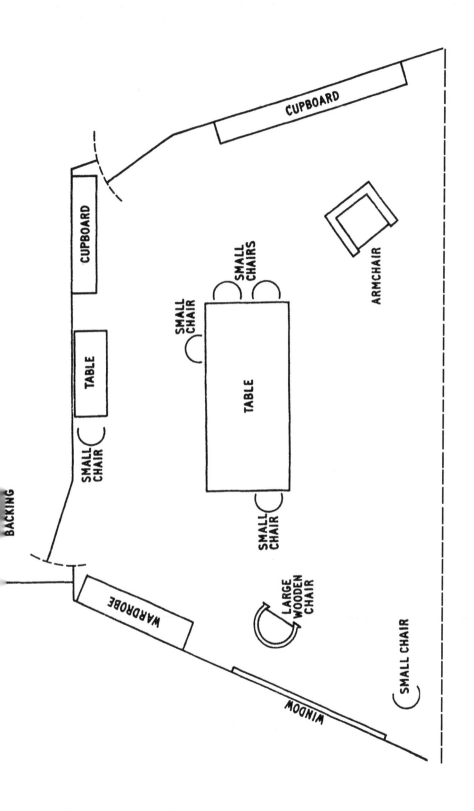

PROPERTY LIST

ACT I

Set:
Small wardrobe by wall, U.R.
In it:
Coats and hats
Small table D.C.
By it:
Small chair
On it:
Notebook and pencil
Book shelf above table with dictionary
Low cupboards against wall, U.L. and D.L.
In cupboards:
Exercise books, papers, text books, etc.
Newspaper on cupboard D.L.
Notice boards above cupboards
Large table C.
On it:
Paper and pencils for five
Pair of spectacles
By it:
Four small chairs
Handsome wooden chair with arms by window R.
Elderly easy chair D.L.
Bottle of ink on window ledge

Offstage L.:
Glass of water (SALLY)
Piles of exercise books (JANE *and* MRS. THORPE)

Offstage R.:
Telephone with long cable
Coat (SALLY)
Handbag (MISS ROWE)
In it:
Newspaper cutting
Gold-capped fountain pen

Personal:
MRS. THORPE
Wristwatch
Small gift in box inside large handbag
JANE
Cigarettes and lighter
MISS ROWE
Prospectus
Paper hanky
MAUDIE
Hanky
HATTY
Walking stick

ACT II

Set:
Curtains open
Big table moved slightly to L.
On table:
Exercise books (MISS DANVERS)
Large settee under window D.R.
On it:
Some large cushions

On table D.C.:
Telephone
Typewriter

Strike:
Glass of water
Spilled ink

Check:
Exercise books in cupboard D.L.

Offstage L.:
Register (MISS DANVERS)
School bell
Tray with six coffee cups (SALLY)

Personal:
MRS. EMMETT

Wristwatch
Handbag with cigarettes and
    lighter
MRS. THORPE
Capacious bag with knitting
SALLY
Compact in pocket
HATTY
Walking stick

ACT III

Set:
Wall behind door U.R., now stripped
    of paper
Check coats and hats in wardrobe
Stencil in typewriter
Books and pencils on large table
JANE's handbag on top of cupboard
    L.
Check key in keyhole of door U.R.
Check cushions on settee

Offstage L.:
Exercise books (MAY *and* JANE)

Offstage R.:
Hammer

Personal:
MRS. THORPE
Pile of black and white 'ghost'
    paintings
SALLY
Armful of registers
MATTY
Old fashioned black reticule con-
    taining gold capped fountain
    pen

Lightning Source UK Ltd.
Milton Keynes UK
UKOW01f0344011117
311964UK00006B/389/P